Communications
in Computer and Information Science 530

Commenced Publication in 2007
Founding and Former Series Editors:
Alfredo Cuzzocrea, Dominik Ślęzak, and Xiaokang Yang

More information about this series at http://www.springer.com/series/7899

Frances Cleary · Massimo Felici (Eds.)

Cyber Security and Privacy

4th Cyber Security and Privacy Innovation Forum,
CSP Innovation Forum 2015
Brussels, Belgium, April 28–29, 2015
Revised Selected Papers

Editors
Frances Cleary
Waterford Institute of Technology
Waterford
Ireland

Massimo Felici
Security and Cloud Lab
Hewlett-Packard Laboratories
Bristol
UK

ISSN 1865-0929   ISSN 1865-0937   (electronic)
Communications in Computer and Information Science
ISBN 978-3-319-25359-6   ISBN 978-3-319-25360-2   (eBook)
DOI 10.1007/978-3-319-25360-2

Library of Congress Control Number: 2015950892

Springer Cham Heidelberg New York Dordrecht London

Printed on acid-free paper

Springer International Publishing AG Switzerland is part of Springer Science+Business Media
(www.springer.com)

Foreword by the European Commission

Utilizing the capability and dynamism of the EU single market, the European Commission supports a Digital Single Market strategy, launched in May 2015, that builds on three main pillars and 16 key actions. "By fostering a Digital Single Market, the EU can create up to €415 billion per year in additional growth, hundreds of thousands of new jobs, and a vibrant knowledge-based society" and actively make a real and tangible difference in the economy, in business, in the daily life of citizens, and in society.

To protect personal data and prevent unauthorized information sharing, gathering, and surveillance in the technological modern society of today, increased security and privacy are essential concerns affecting the digital single market that have expressed by practitioners, policy makers, and experts over the last several years. Cyberattacks may have potential catastrophic impacts on the economy and society, hence a strategically focused effort and commitment to work to reduce such risks is being implemented at the EU level to address emerging vulnerabilities.

With more devices and smart technologies being adopted and exploited by European citizens, companies, organizations, and SMEs in their daily activities, businesses, private and social activities (at home), online accessible services and infrastructures need to be better protected, so as to actively increase the level of online trust and to have further positive economic impact.

Trust and security in the digital world is core to the European Digital Single Market. The Network and Information Security (NIS) Directive aims to ensure a high common level of cybersecurity in the European Union. This will be achieved by improving Member States' national cybersecurity capabilities, by improving cooperation between Member States and by improving cooperation between public and private sectors. Also, companies in critical sectors – such as energy, transport, banking, and health – as well as key Internet services will be required to adopt risk management best practices and report major incidents to the national authorities.

A proposal of "a partnership with the industry on cybersecurity in the area of technologies and solutions for online network security" (Key Action 13, Pillar III) is specifically relevant to the European Commission's cybersecurity strategy. The cybersecurity PPP is expected to mobilize public and private resources in order to stimulate the supply of innovative cybersecurity products and services in Europe. The cybersecurity PPP is expected to be established in the first half of 2016.

In order to reinforce trust and security in digital services, notably concerning the handling of personal data and the protection of privacy in the electronic communications sector, the European Commission will also review the e-Privacy Directive, building on the soon to be adopted EU Data Protection Regulation.

To support such important initiatives all actors from the trust and security community need to come together to actively and visibly demonstrate, promote, and embrace cutting-edge and innovative research outputs and success stories, drawing attention to the ground-breaking innovation coming from FP7 and pursued in different pillars of H2020 as a key focus area.

The Cybersecurity and Privacy (CSP) Innovation Forum 2015, organized and successfully executed in close collaboration between the CSP Forum and the European commission DG CONNECT (Unit H4 Trust and Security), was a unique two-day event showcasing more than 40 top technical, trust and security research projects, highlighting state-of-the-art and innovative research in focus areas such as cryptography, cloud security, trustworthy network and service infrastructures, and mobile device technologies and tools. A distinctive wider security community of delegates from European-based security-focused initiatives, policy makers, industry representatives (large and SME), and leading experts and research academics attended this event, clearly conveying the high priority given to R&I activities in this domain. They called for further investment and focus on innovative cybersecurity outputs to maintain European competitiveness in this domain.

This two-day event included topical cybersecurity track sessions and also a focused session dealing specifically with the Network and Information Security Directive (NIS), providing an overview of the key targeted areas that are expected to contribute to the higher level of cybersecurity in Europe.

The NIS directive is currently being negotiated within the European Parliament and the Council and is expected to be adopted before the end of the year.

Collaboration, networking, and community building are a necessary building block to combat the ongoing cybersecurity issues we as a society are faced with. Having the Cybersecurity and Privacy (CSP) Forum as a main platform for such engagement is vital to the continued dissemination, awareness raising, and the creation of valuable synergies to allow experts come together, to work as a community, to join forces to address these ongoing concerns. Striving for a safer online environment and safer society for our future generations.

August 2015

Jakub Boratynski
Head of Unit
DG CONNECT
European Commission

Foreword by Seccord

The CSP Forum initiative[1] (funded by the EU FP7 SecCord[2] CSA project) has a core objective of enabling enhanced collaboration through effective clustering of EU-funded trust and security research projects. Funded research projects contribute to the larger work program of the commission. The CSP forum, through its promotion of collaboration, encourages trust- and security-focused projects to work to create synergies, coming together as a community for greater impact.

A core activity of the CSP Forum initiative is the organization of an annual cybersecurity and privacy innovation forum conference, widening the outreach and dissemination of the success stories and innovations to a wider community. The proceedings from the Annual Cyber Security and Privacy (CSP) Innovation Forum Conference 2015[3] are included in this volume. The CSP Innovation Forum 2015 was organized by the European Commission, DG CNECT (Unit H4 Trust & Security), and the CSP Forum (supported by A4CLOUD, ATTPS, IPACSO, PRIPARE, SECCORD, SECURED, TREsPASS).

This important two-day event provided a unique opportunity for like-minded industry professionals, academics, policy makers, and business investors to come together for fruitful networking opportunities and to showcase real cyber security and privacy research success stories, future upcoming challenges/research priorities, and opportunities for investment stemming from mature research activities. Over 40 top technical trust and security research project demonstrators and innovative outputs were on display in the dedicated exhibition booths at the event over the two days. The CSP Innovation Forum Conference 2015 consisted of the following main key activities:

- H2020-focused work program informational sessions
- Unique opportunities for networking with industry, policy makers, researchers, investors
- Overview of the EC trust and security research portfolio and innovative success stories
- Variety of technical and hot topical track sessions in the cybersecurity and privacy domain
- Meet and interact with the researchers at the core of the current state-of-the-art research-funded projects, availing of the opportunity to link with them and see live demonstrators in the main exhibition areas
- Find out more about current policies in the making and future EC cybersecurity strategies

---

[1] https://www.cspforum.eu/

[2] http://www.seccord.eu/

[3] https://www.cspforum.eu/2015

Horizon 2020 (H2020)[4], an EU flagship initiative aimed at securing Europe's global competitiveness, actively works to couple research and innovation with a core goal of ensuring that Europe produces world-class science, removing existing barriers to innovation, providing an environment for both private and public sectors to come together for greater impact. The CSP forum through its ongoing activities aligns itself with the H2020 objective and innovation/impact focus by:

1. Providing an overview of the EU trust and security research portfolio (focusing on outputs/success stories with real marketable impact/potential)
2. Addressing policy in the making; assessing funded project activities and their relation to the cybersecurity strategy; "Impact on Europe"; EU data protection reform; "protecting your personal data/privacy"
3. Assessing economic barriers of trust and security technology uptake; how to access the market more effectively; research on Industry impact; how to improve, implement and succeed
4. Aligning Trust and Security EU initiatives with focused Member state initiatives – 'Investigating How to work together better'.

The CSP Forum is a valuable initiative supporting the dissemination, promotion, and uptake of innovation coming from funded trust- and security-focused projects that welcomes continued collaboration and networking with interested experts in this exciting and challenging research domain.

June 2015   Frances Cleary
                                                    SecCord Project Coordinator

---

[4] http://ec.europa.eu/programmes/horizon2020/

Preface

This volume consists of the selected revised papers based on the presentations at the Cyber Security and Privacy (CSP) Innovation Forum 2015 held in Brussels, Belgium, during April 28–29, 2015. The CSP Innovation Forum 2015 was organized in collaboration with the European Commission, DG CONNECT (Unit H4 Trust & Security). The event included DG CONNECT H2020 informational sessions relating to "Digital Security: Cybersecurity, Privacy, and Trust" calls in 2015.

This volume builds on the experiences of the previous edited CSP Forum editions (published by Springer as CCIS 182 and CCIS 470). It is edited with the intention and ambition to develop and establish a "portfolio" of European research. The main objective is to support the dissemination and visibility of research outcomes beyond research communities to various stakeholders (e.g., researchers, practitioners, and policy-makers) by proving a collection of research contributions funded by European Commission's research and innovation programs. The edited proceedings of the annual editions of the CSP Forum capture the evolution of research and innovation in cyber security and privacy in Europe.

This volume contains on-going research activities and results carried out within European projects mostly funded by the European Commission's research and innovation programs. The conference program consisted of two official opening plenary sessions and 20 different tracks involving a variety of presentations and panel discussions covering the key challenges and strategies available to effectively manage employee, citizen, and corporate trust. The conference provided an opportunity for those in business, the public sector, research, and government who are involved in the policy, security, systems, and processes surrounding security and privacy technologies. The papers collected in this volume received support from organizations, national research programs, and the European Commission's research and innovation programs, in particular, by the following EU projects (in alphabetical order):

- A4CLOUD
  Accountability for Cloud and Other Future Internet Services
  FP7-317550
- Coco Cloud
  Confidential and Compliant Clouds
  FP7-610853
- INTER-TRUST
  Interoperable Trust Assurance Infrastructure
  FP7-317731
- IPACSO
  Innovation Framework for Privacy and Cyber Security Market Opportunities
  FP7-609892

- MASSIF
  Management of Security Information and Events in Service Infrastructures
  FP7-257475
- OpenI
  Open-Source, Web-Based, Framework for Integrating Applications with Cloud-Based Services and Personal Cloudlets.
  FP7-317883
- OPTET
  OPerational Trustworthiness Enabling Technologies
  FP7-317631
- PRIPARE
  Preparing Industry to Privacy-by-Design by Supporting Its Application in Research
  FP7-610613
- PRISMACLOUD
  Privacy and Security Maintaining Services in the Cloud
  H2020-644962
- SECURED
  Security at the Network Edge
  FP7-611458

The CSP Innovation Forum 2015 received support from the following EU projects:

- A4CLOUD
- ATTPS
  Achieving the Trust Paradigm Shift
  FP7-317665
- IPACSO
- PRIPARE
- SecCord
  Security and Trust Coordination and Enhanced Collaboration
  FP7-316622
- SECURED
- TREsPASS
  Technology-Supported Risk Estimation by Predictive Assessment of Socio technical Security
  FP7- 318003

This two-day conference organized by the SecCord project had invited presenters, panellists, and exhibitors to contribute to this collection of selected papers. Two types of papers were solicited to be published in the proceedings of the conference:

- Practical Experience Reports and Tools, presenting in-depth description of practitioner experiences, case studies, and tools
- Research Papers, presenting recent original research results providing new insights to the community

The submissions were peer-reviewed by three Program Committee members and experts. The peer-review process provided authors with valuable feedback in order to improve their papers. The selected papers grouped into thematic parts of these proceedings offer just a snapshot of the two-day conference, which provided an opportunity to present and debate on going cyber security and privacy research and development in Europe. These proceedings intend to inform researchers, practitioners, and policy-makers about research developments and technological opportunities for innovation in cyber security and privacy.

We would like to thank everyone who made the publication of these proceedings possible, in particular the authors, the Program Committee members and reviewers, the conference organizers, and the supporting organizations.

June 2015

Frances Cleary
Massimo Felici
CSP Innovation Forum 2015 Chairs

Organization

Organizing Committee

Michele Bezzi	SAP, France
Gerard Blom	Bicore, The Netherlands
Diarmaid Brennan	Waterford Institute of Technology, Ireland
Frances Cleary	Waterford Institute of Technology, Ireland
Luca Compagna	SAP, France
Zeta Dooly	Waterford Institute of Technology, Ireland
Massimo Felici	HP Labs, UK
Margaret Ford	Consult Hyperion, UK
Antonio Kung	Trialog, France
Antonio Lioy	Politecnico di Torino, Italy
Fabio Massacci	University of Trento, Italy
Rodrigo Mendes	European Commission, DG CONNECT, Unit H4, EU
Martin Muehleck	European Commission, DG CONNECT, Unit H4, EU
Aljosa Pasic	ATOS, Spain
Andrzej Verissimo Szeremeta	European Commission, DG CONNECT, Unit H4, EU
Nick Wainwright	HP Labs, UK

Program Committee Members and Reviewers

Frances Cleary, Ireland (Chair)
Massimo Felici, UK (Chair)
Claudio Agostino Ardagna, Italy
Karin Bernsmed, Norway
Diarmaid Brennan, Ireland
Valentina Casola, Italy
Jorge Cuellar, Germany
Ernesto Damiani, Italy
Alessandra De Benedictis, Italy
Michela D'Errico, Italy
Francesco Di Cerbo, France
Olga Gadyatskaya, Luxembourg
Dina Hadziosmanovic, The Netherlands
Mario Hoffmann, Germany
Dharm Kapletia, UK
Diego Lopez, Spain
Evangelos Markatos, Greece

Fabio Martinelli, Italy
Stefano Paraboschi, Italy
Aljosa Pasic, Spain
Erkuden Rios, Spain
Antonio Gómez Skarmeta, Spain
Yannis Stamatiou, Greece
Santiago Suppan, Germany
Vasilios Tountopoulos, Greece

Contents

Research and Innovation in Cyber Security and Privacy

Security and Privacy in the Cloud

Implementing Privacy Policies in the Cloud

Claudio Caimi[1], Michela D'Errico[2(✉)], Carmela Gambardella[1],
Mirko Manea[1], and Nick Wainwright[2]

[1] HP Italiana S.r.l., Milan, Italy
[2] HP Labs, Bristol, UK
Michela.derrico@hp.com

Abstract. The provision of a cloud service must fulfil policies to comply with requirements coming from different sources. One of the main sources is the European Data Protection Directive that sets out legal obligations for the cloud adoption and provision. Cloud providers that rely on the use of additional cloud services need to make sure that the level of protection offered by these is adequate. Implementing privacy policies in the cloud requires taking into account the privacy related practices adopted by service providers even during the procurement phase. Moving towards a transparency-based service provision approach, additional information that cloud customers need to evaluate is evidence of compliance with privacy policies that CSPs are able to provide. This paper gives an overview of the processes entailed for the implementation of privacy policies.

Keywords: Privacy policy · Privacy level agreement · Data Sharing Agreement · Policy enforcement

1 Introduction

Cloud providers need to implement privacy policies in order to comply with requirements derived from different sources, including business rules and contractual obligations. Among the main sources of requirements is the Data Protection Directive 95/46/EC (DPD) [1], which sets out the obligations that Cloud Service Providers (CSPs) have to fulfil with regard to the processing of personal data. CSPs put in place measures to comply with the legal obligations and disclose them in the privacy policy published along with the service description.

This paper takes into account a process view of implementing privacy policies. This view involves a broad process that starts when the provider engages with other service providers for offering their service to the final customers. DPD highlights different responsibilities for Data Controller (DC) and Data Processor (DP). These responsibilities need to be understood in the context of a cloud service provision. The DC is the liable and responsible entity towards the final customers for the provision of a service complying with legal obligations. It is then crucial for a DC to be able to assess the level of data protection offered by prospective providers to be commissioned. The correct implementation of privacy policies is not just in the hands of the DC, but it also depends on the measures adopted by the involved service providers. DCs, when selecting the most suitable provider to use, also needs to evaluate to what degree they

© Springer International Publishing Switzerland 2015
F. Cleary and M. Felici (Eds.): CSP Forum 2015, CCIS 530, pp. 3–13, 2015.
DOI: 10.1007/978-3-319-25360-2_1

will be able to correctly implement privacy policy if they choose a specific service provider. DCs need to find a service with an offered privacy policy that allows them to fulfil the privacy policy they wish to offer to the final customer.

Disclosure of privacy and data protection practices are made by CSPs to (potential) customers in a Privacy Level Agreement (PLA) [2]. When a specific CSP is selected, DC and DP put into writing the agreement about the privacy policy, specifically Data Sharing Agreement (DSA) [4] can be entered into.

This paper gives an overview of the different aspects that CSP have to take into account for the implementation of privacy policies. It describes a typical cloud service provision environment, with the components needed to implement the policy by adopting an accountable-based approach. Through an example of privacy policy statement concerned with the data transfer obligation the paper clarifies the importance of assessing the data protection level offered by CSPs. PLA is introduced to show how information disclosed therein can be exploited by tools to help customers in their service selection task. PLA statements related to the selected service can then be included in a DSA to formalize the agreement terms.

2 On Privacy Policies in the Cloud

Organisations use legal documents (contracts) to specify the terms and conditions under which they agree to share data among themselves or with users. The policies expressed in such contracts remain inaccessible from the software infrastructure supporting the data sharing and management processes. They still need to be interpreted and translated (primarily by humans) into meaningful technical policies and constraints, to ensure degrees of enforcement and auditing.

Often end-users are asked to accept online a series of legal and contractual clauses (usually they are called "Terms and Conditions") which are not so clear to understand and this implies an inability to decline particular aspects of them if the user wants to use the service. Moreover, the user is not able to verify if these rules are properly respected by the organisation: violation detections require verification of organisational practices, auditing and accountability frameworks.

From a legal and technical perspective, initial work in these areas has been carried out in various R&D projects and initiatives, including W3C P3P [13], IBM EPAL work [14], PRIME [9], PrimeLife [10] and Consequence [11]. For example, mechanisms regulating end-users' privacy preferences on personal data, sticky policies, and external auditing trust authorities have been introduced [12] to ensure that confidential data is protected during the sharing process, that access to data by organisations is constrained and subject to the fulfilment of specific management and enforcement steps, and degrees of assurance and accountability are provided.

A4Cloud [5] and Coco Cloud [6] projects have conducted research on PLA and DSA in order to introduce them as means that can be used to specify, disclose and implement privacy policies. Managing the lifecycle of privacy policies, from their specification to their enforcement and the detection of their violation is, in fact, a core objective for A4Cloud project. A4Cloud project has been developing a set of tools enabling an accountability based-approach in managing policies. At the enforcement level of the privacy policies lifecycle, A4Cloud has designed and developed an engine denoted as A-PPLE [23]. This engine has been specifically designed to put in effect policies while also producing the evidence needed to assess the compliance of the actions performed. The A-PPLE is able to process and enforce policies specified through the policy language denoted as A-PPL [24].

Coco Cloud project has been conducting research on the same area of the policy definition and enforcement with the aim to develop tools able to manage the lifecycle of the DSA. In particular, for the policy definition area, Coco Cloud has been finalizing the development of an authoring tool to support the creation of electronic, human readable DSAs [17]. For the enforcement part, Coco Cloud has also been working on the development of an engine similar to the A-PPLE, focused on the handling of legal obligations and authorisations [18], especially tailored for the cloud environment. Coco Cloud plans to develop an enforcement engine usable on OpenStack™ [22], in particular to apply data protection to its object storage service (Swift [25]).

With regards to the policy specification language, Coco Cloud has designed the CocoEPL language able to express temporal intervals when applying policies, as well as usage control obligations in terms of event and condition-based triggers. CocoEPL merges and relies on former works like U-XACML [19] and PPL [20]. The mentioned engines are able to process policies written in languages that have been built on top of standard extendable languages as XACML [21].

In the following sections we introduce data protection roles before dealing with PLA and DSA agreements.

2.1 Cloud and Data Protection Roles

In a cloud environment, distinguishing between DC and DP is not always so clear-cut because it is context-dependent. Generally speaking, cloud providers are considered as processors of cloud-processed data so far as the provider adheres to the instructions of the DC and does not process the data for its own purpose. However, cloud providers might be considered joint-controllers under certain circumstances [3].

Ultimately, cloud providers are DCs about the user-related personal data processed for their own purposes. However, the decision regarding the legal status of cloud providers on the cloud-processed data remains context dependent owing to the extent of their involvement in determining the purpose and means of processing. For example, infrastructure providers are often considered as DP as long as they follow the instructions of the DC in processing the personal data.

A DC must choose a DP which is able to guarantee appropriate security measures for the data protection; the DP is any person or organisation who processes the data on behalf of the DC. The DC is responsible for the security of the personal data and the protection of its integrity, therefore, when it comes to decide the DPs to engage with, the CSP will most likely choose the DP that has adopted an accountable approach in carrying out its processing tasks.

2.2 Privacy Level Agreement

PLA is a standard developed by Cloud Security Alliance (CSA) to structure information related to data protection and privacy related practices. CSPs disclose in PLA information about how they fulfil the legal obligations set out in the Data Protection Directive 95/46/EC [1]. PLA is a natural language agreement in which CSP disclose the practices they adopt to be compliant with the law. The agreement is structured into sections, each one pertaining to a specific aspect to be addressed to comply with the obligations set out by the DPD. Examples of aspects taken into account are: the ways the personal data are processed, details about the data transfer (such as the countries where data will be processed), the measures in place to ensure security properties such as availability, integrity and confidentiality, how data retention, deletion and termination are handled.

The standardized structure enables the comparison of PLA associated to different providers and cloud services. Yet the comparison is an activity that has to be performed by humans who read and compare the content of the proposed PLA, section by section. There may be hundreds of services available, in this case a manual (i.e. human-performed) comparison is not manageable and should be minimized. Customers may benefit from tools that can help them to filter suitable services based on the requirements over the data protection and privacy practices. To enable tools to perform this type of first selection, PLA content has to be structured and possible practices options categorized so that a machine readable representation can be designed. This is the approach that we have taken to turn PLA into a software exploitable tool [26]. Even though the nature of the content handled is different, this approach is very close to the approach followed by several works done around the Service Level Agreement (SLA) [7]. The idea is always to automate many of the human-performed tasks in order to achieve efficiency.

2.3 Data Sharing Agreement

An electronic Data Sharing Agreement (e-DSA) is a human-readable, yet machine-processable contract, regulating how organizations and/or individuals share data. Sharing data among groups of organizations and/or individuals is essential in a modern cloud-based service provision, being at the very core of scientific and business transactions [8]. Data sharing, however, poses several problems including trust, privacy, data misuse and/or abuse, and uncontrolled propagation of data.

A DSA can be established between two organisations and/or individuals (bilateral agreement), or more (multilateral agreement). DSA can also be adopted to share information inside an organisation, between its different business units.

A DSA consists of:

- Predefined legal background information (which is usually available from a template, following, e.g., the textual template of traditional legal contracts). A subject matter expert (e.g., company lawyer) provides such description most of the times. This kind of information is unstructured by nature, that is information that is not organized in a predefined manner.

- Structured user-defined information, including the definition of the validity period, the parties participating in the agreement, the data covered and, most importantly, the statements that constrain how data can be shared among the parties (such statements usually include policy rules). Business policy experts and end users define and implement these fields.

When a DSA regulates access and usage of personal data, it usually involves DC, DP, and Data Subject. Two DCs stipulate a DSA in order to agree with the data usage and to establish duties of each of the parties in relation to the data sharing: it might include a section dedicated to the privacy policies definition. The DCs participate in the responsibilities either equally, with different degrees or at different stages.

The agreement defines how to access the data, the nature of the data involved, the purpose of the data processing, the time interval in which the contract is valid and a set of rules to obey to for the involved parties. Furthermore, it can include responsibilities for the data management even after the contract is no longer in place, for instance, upon contract expiration, all data must be destroyed or returned to the DC. Specific constraints can be required concerning features, quality, and characteristics of the data. The Data Subject is the owner of the data and s/he can be involved to specify preferences or to provide additional information in the policies definition.

According to the DSA, the DC which wants to use the services provided by a cloud provider will evaluate services which offer privacy level agreements that show data management processes compliant with the DSA definition.

3 Privacy Policies in Cloud Service Provision

Actors involved in a cloud service provision assume different roles according to the processing of personal data. Based on the role, the degree of responsibility changes and different governance issues need to be addressed. It is important to identify the Data Controller as it determines the actor who has to comply with the DPD. To achieve compliance, the Data Controller has to assess the policies put in place by the different DPs delegated to perform specific data processing tasks over the personal data the Data Controller has been entrusted with. Compliance with DPD principles not only protects data subjects' rights, but also reflects good business practices in place, which contribute to reliable and efficient data processing.

An example of service supply chain involves an organisation with the role of Data Controller and two service providers with the role of Data Processors. The Data Controller has to comply with a set of principles, among which the principle concerned with the data transfer. This principle requires the Data Controller not to send data to a non-European Economic Area country which does not ensure an adequate level of protection (exceptions to comply with this principle exist). The Data Controller is the entity liable in case the data are transferred to a country which is not deemed as a country offering adequate protection. Moreover, the Data Controller wants to be sure that the services that it will use as components for its own service, provide the required guarantees. Data Controller, in the role of customer, has to select cloud service components taking into account this data transfer related requirement. In this case, specifically, what the customer needs to know is whether the service being selected will transfer data, which is the entity and the country receiving the data, the motivations for the data transfer (it may be for regular operations or for emergency). Data Controller needs to evaluate the strength of the safeguards put in place by the CSPs involved in its own service provision to be able to comply with data protection requirements [15]. Gathering key information needed for performing the assessment about the adequacy of the safeguards in place is a feature that customers may benefit from during their decision-making phase.

3.1 Service Procurement

PLA and DSA, in their machine readable versions, can be exploited during the service procurement phase. During this phase a customer evaluates the offerings of a set of available services against its own requirements. The results of this phase will be the subset of services that match the customer's needs. This scenario is depicted in Fig. 1.

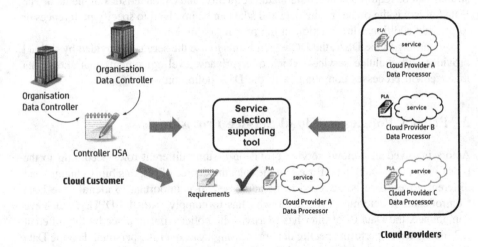

Fig. 1. Privacy policy-driven service selection

Let us consider the simplest example of a Data Controller that wishes to offer a service whose target customers care about the data transfer policy and will likely prefer to use a service whose data processing tasks are carried out within the European Economic Area (EEA). Data transfers within EEA countries are actually allowed by the DPD without further additional restrictions.

During the service procurement face Data Controller faces the problem of selecting a service that carries out data processing tasks in locations within EEA. The services available for the selection will have an accompanying PLA in which, among others, data transfer policy is stated. The policy statement about the data transfer will specify whether data may need to be transferred across borders, the reasons for this transfer (e.g. emergency or regular service operations), the location where data will be transferred and the legal ground allowing it (e.g., Binding Corporate Rules, model contracts). As the DC is specifically searching for a DP handling data within EEA, the data transfer sections of the PLA associated to the available services will be analysed to extract the information needed. The tool supporting the decision making of the DC takes into account the requirement that data transfer has to be done within EEA and, after analysing the PLAs, will provide the DC a list of services complying with this requirement.

Data Controller is the entity responsible and liable towards the customers, therefore, in addition to checking the constraint about data transfer occurring in EEA, he may also want to check the means by which the Data Processor can prove that the data transfer restriction is being fulfilled.

A tool that can support the DC in this phase has been developed within A4Cloud. This tool, the Cloud Offerings Advisory Tool [16], can help DC to select by presenting a list of questions whose answers constitute the set of requirements that the desired service has to meet.

Once the Data Processor has been identified, a DSA is created to formalize the statements about the data sharing between the Data Controller and the Data Processor. If no changes to data transfer section need to be negotiated, DSA is envisaged to contain a DSA compliant representation of relevant sections in the PLA. In our example, the data transfer statement will be part of the DSA.

3.2 Implementing Privacy Policy

Once agreements have been signed up, CSPs taking part in the cloud service chain need to set up their IT infrastructure, software and services so that the terms of the agreements can be fulfilled.

The overall process of the policy implementation can be structured into three main phases: policy definition, policy enforcement and monitoring. Carrying out each one of these phases may involve actors with different expertise and thus different sets of tools are to be used.

The policy definition phase has the goal to define the set of the policies adopted by the CSP. During this phase legal experts and policy experts analyse the requirements set by internal (such as business rules) and external criteria (such as the compliance with the law) and, as a result of this phase, a set of policies fulfilling those requirements is specified. This set of policies would be made available to interested stakeholders that need to evaluate their appropriateness against their needs. Tools typically used during this phase include tools that analyse the external and internal criteria and suggest the best way to meet those. To help actors with the concrete task of writing policies, authoring tools, such as the one being developed within Coco Cloud, can be used. This tools have a Graphical User Interface (GUI) that supports the writing of clauses by providing information about the context and templates to customise. The result of this phase is therefore a human readable document that a CSP that enters into a contract with a customer has to put in effect. The CSP needs then to plan the enforcement of the policies defined, that may involve or not tasks carried out by people. For policy clauses to be performed by tools, we want to enable software components to enforce and monitor the compliance of the service provision with the privacy policies. To this end these latter need to be implemented at software level and linked with the policy statements. This goal is achieved by translating privacy policy statements into a set of machine readable and enforceable policies that are then fed to the software components.

Based on the capabilities of the enforcement components deployed in the cloud provision environment, different languages may be used. A4Cloud and Coco Cloud projects have developed two enforcement components that take as input policies represented in two different technical policy languages.

The expressiveness of the language, on one hand, and its comprehensibility, on the other, is a problem addressed by Coco Cloud project and solved by introducing a Controlled Natural Language (CNL), which allows to express policies in a processable but, at the same time, quite human readable way. Nevertheless, a gap between the expressiveness of the language and the enforceability of the rules still exists: not everything that is expressible is necessarily enforceable.

The translation of declared policies into their enforceable representation can be automated by creating an ontology-based representation of the PLA statements. This automation feature allows to achieve efficiency in the creation of machine level policies and to keep track of the link between policy statements and software means used for their enforcement. The machine readable version is then enriched by including, for each statement, the information about the enforcement components used and the software artifact produced for each policy statements, as schematically illustrated in Fig. 2. This mapping across different abstraction layers can be used to get information about how the CSP plans to achieve the objectives stated in the policy documents.

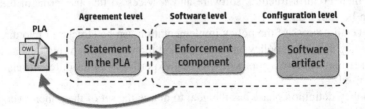

Fig. 2. Representation of policies at different abstraction levels

The first step required for the implementation of privacy policies is the definition of policies in (controlled) natural language. The subsequent step is the representation of the policies in a machine readable format that can enable further elaboration of the policy statements. The elaboration the projects aim to achieve is the automatic translation of the policies into a representation that enables their enforcement through specific tools like the mentioned engines. There are policy statements that cannot be enforced by the means of software tools as human intervention is needed to perform actions. In this case it is important to have a machine readable representation as it can be analysed to check the policies declared against the policies desired by customers. Other types of policies can be enforced, but the evidence that can be produced does not provide the level of assurance that may be required to demonstrate compliance with the policies declared. An example of policy statement with these characteristics is the data retention policy, in which CSPs declare for how long personal data will be retained and what happens when the data retention expires. Typically, when the period for retention expires, the privacy agreement foresees the secure deletion of the data. Software can be configured so that data are deleted by using an irretrievable method and a notification is sent to the interested party informing that data have been deleted. However we recognize that a complete understanding of the status of the data deletion result is difficult to achieve. We reckon though that having set up tools that delete and send notification, and being able to show the existence of the tools set up, is a step further than just declaring that a deletion policy has been adopted.

Accountable service providers need not only to correctly define policies and set up the components in charge of their enforcement. They also have to deploy components delegated to monitor and log events occurring during the service provision, in order to be able to demonstrate that components are running as agreed and expected. Accountable CSPs have also to design and deploy components able to process evidence and detect violations. In case of violation, an accountable approach also require to send notifications to the effected actors, so that the appropriate countermeasures or remediation actions can be taken.

Figure 3 shows the different phases that the implementation of privacy policies entails for a CSP adopting an accountability-based approach. A key element, upon which an accountable provision can be built, is the production of evidence as a proof that processes are running according to the signed policy.

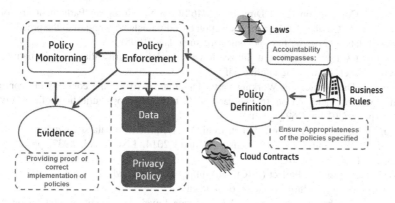

Fig. 3. Implementation of privacy policy

4   Conclusions

Cloud actors taking part in a service provision chain have different responsibilities with respect to the data processing tasks they perform. A DC is the entity liable towards the data subjects for implementing the privacy policies disclosed and agreed. DC can involve different service providers in the provision of his own service. The choices he makes about the specific services to use may affect his ability to comply with requirements about data protection and privacy, as the final privacy policy he is able to implement also depends on the privacy policy adopted by prospective Data Processors.

A4Cloud and Coco Cloud projects have been conducting research on the use of PLA and DSA within tools supporting the customers to make the best decision. Work is being carried out to include into these machine readable agreements information about the enforcement and monitoring components set up and the evidence that can be produced. In fact, moving towards an accountability-based approach, cloud customers will likely prefer to use cloud providers which offer also evidence-based assurance that the right processes have been put in place. Cloud providers need then to set up IT infrastructures and software components for the cloud service provision which allow the production and provision of evidence to be used by accountable actors to prove that privacy policy is being implemented as agreed. In fact, machine readable policy statements enable the mapping with the correspondent enforcement level representations. Furthermore, this link between different abstraction levels allows to trace evidence and its analysis result (such as a violation) back to the policy statements whose enforcement has produced that evidence.

Acknowledgments.   This work has been partially funded from the European Commission's Seventh Programme (FP7/2007-2013) under grant agreements no. 317550 (A4CLOUD) and no. 610853 (Coco Cloud).

References

1. European Commission (EC): Directive 95/46/EC of the European Parliament and of the Council of 24 October 1995 on the protection of individuals with regard to the processing of personal data and on the free movement of such data (1995)
2. CSA Privacy Level Agreement. https://downloads.cloudsecurityalliance.org/initiatives/pla/Privacy_Level_Agreement_Outline.pdf
3. Article 29 Data Protection Working Party: Opinion 1/2010 on the concepts of "controller and processor", adopted on 16 February 2010. http://ec.europa.eu/justice/policies/privacy/docs/wpdocs/2010/wp169_en.pdf
4. Egea, M., Matteucci, I., Mori, P., Petrocchi, M.: Definition of data sharing agreements. In: Felici, M., Fernández-Gago, C. (eds.) A4Cloud 2014. LNCS, vol. 8937, pp. 248–272. Springer, Heidelberg (2015)
5. Cloud Accountability Project (A4CLoud). http://www.a4cloud.eu/
6. Coco Cloud Project. http://www.coco-cloud.eu/
7. Patel, P., Ranabahu, A.H., Sheth, A.P.: Service Level Agreement in Cloud Computing (2009)
8. Casassa-Mont, M., Matteucci, I., Petrocchi, M., Sbodio, M.L.: Towards safer information sharing in the Cloud. Int. J. Inf. Secur. **14**, 1–16 (2014)
9. EU PRIME Project. www.prime-project.eu/
10. EU PrimeLife Project. http://primelife.ercim.eu/
11. EU Consequence Project, Context-aware Data-centric Information Sharing. www.consequence-project.eu/
12. Pearson, S., Casassa-Mont, M.: Sticky policies: An approach for managing privacy across multiple parties. IEEE Comput. **44**(9), 60–68 (2011). IEEE
13. Platform for Privacy Preferences Project, (P3P). www.w3.org/P3P/

14. Enterprise Privacy Authorization Language (EPAL 1.2). http://www.zurich.ibm.com/security/enterprise-privacy/epal/Specification
15. Information Commissioners Office: Assessing Adequacy - International transfers of personal data (2012). https://ico.org.uk/media/for-organisations/documents/1529/assessing_adequacy_international_data_transfers.pdf
16. Alnemr, R., Pearson, S., Leenes, R., Mhungu, R.: COAT: cloud offerings advisory tool. In: 2014 IEEE 6th International Conference on Cloud Computing Technology and Science (CloudCom), pp. 95–100. IEEE (2014)
17. Manea, M., Petrocchi, M.: Engineering the lifecycle of data sharing agreements. ERCIM News **100**, 20–21 (2015)
18. Di Cerbo, F., Some, D.F., Gomez, L., Trabelsi, S.: PPL v2.0: uniform data access and usage control on cloud and mobile. In: TELERISE - 1st International Workshop on TEchnical and LEgal aspects of data pRIvacy and Security, Affiliated workshop with ICSE (2015)
19. Colombo, M., Lazouski, A., Martinelli, F., Mori, P.: A proposal on enhancing XACML with continuous Usage Control features. In: Desprez, F., Getov, V., Priol, T., Yahyapour, R. (eds.) Proceedings of CoreGRID ERCIM Working Group Workshop on Grids, P2P and Services Computing, pp. 133–146. Springer, Heidelberg (2010)
20. Trabelsi, S., Njeh, A., Bussard, L., Neven, G.: PPL engine: A symmetric architecture for privacy policy handling. In: W3C Workshop on Privacy and Data Usage Control **4**(5) (2010)
21. OASIS XACML TC. eXtensible Access Control Markup Language (XACML) Version 3.0 (2010)
22. OpenStack Open Source Cloud Computing Software. https://www.openstack.org/
23. Azraoui, M., Elkhiyaoui, K., Önen, M., Bernsmed, K., De Oliveira, A.S., Sendor, J.: A-PPL: an accountability policy language. In: Garcia-Alfaro, J., Herrera-Joancomartí, J., Lupu, E., Posegga, J., Aldini, A., Martinelli, F., Suri, N. (eds.) DPM/SETOP/QASA 2014. LNCS, vol. 8872, pp. 319–326. Springer, Heidelberg (2015)
24. Azraoui, M., Elkhiyaoui, K., Önen, M., Bernsmed, K., de Oliveira, S., Anderson, Sendor, J.: A-PPL: An accountability policy language. EURECOM Research Report RR-14-294 (2014). http://www.eurecom.fr/publication/4372
25. Swift's documentation. http://docs.openstack.org/developer/swift/
26. D'Errico, M., Pearson, S.: Towards a Formalised Representation for the technical enforcement of privacy level agreements. In: Proceedings of the IEEE 1st International Workshop on Legal and Technical Issues in Cloud Computing (CLaw), pp. 422–427

Towards a New Paradigm for Privacy and Security in Cloud Services

Thomas Lorünser[1]([✉]), Charles Bastos Rodriguez[2], Denise Demirel[3],
Simone Fischer-Hübner[4], Thomas Groß[5], Thomas Länger[6], Mathieu des Noes[7],
Henrich C. Pöhls[8], Boris Rozenberg[9], and Daniel Slamanig[10]

[1] AIT Austrian Institute of Technology, Vienna, Austria
thomas.loruenser@ait.ac.at
[2] ATOS Spain S.A., Madrid, Spain
[3] Technische Universität Darmstadt, Darmstadt, Germany
[4] Karlstad University, Karlstad, Sweden
[5] Newcastle University, Newcastle upon Tyne, UK
[6] University of Lausanne, Lausanne, Switzerland
[7] Commissariat á l'énergie atomique et aux énergies alternatives, Grenoble, France
[8] University of Passau, Passau, Germany
[9] IBM Haifa Research Lab, Haifa, Israel
[10] Graz University of Technology, Graz, Austria

Abstract. The market for cloud computing can be considered as the major growth area in ICT. However, big companies and public authorities are reluctant to entrust their most sensitive data to external parties for storage and processing. The reason for their hesitation is clear: There exist no satisfactory approaches to adequately protect the data during its lifetime in the cloud. The EU Project PRISMACLOUD (Horizon 2020 programme; duration 2/2015–7/2018) addresses these challenges and yields a portfolio of novel technologies to build security enabled cloud services, guaranteeing the required security with the strongest notion possible, namely by means of cryptography. We present a new approach towards a next generation of security and privacy enabled services to be deployed in only partially trusted cloud infrastructures.

1 A New Take on Cloud Security

1.1 Introduction

Today, cloud computing is already omnipresent and starts pervading all aspects of our life, whether in the private area or in the business domain. The annual market value related to cloud computing is estimated to be in the region of USD 150 billion, and will probably grow by the year 2018 to around USD 200 billion [36,41]. The European Commission (EC) promotes in its strategy Digital Agenda for Europe/Europe 2020 the rapid adoption of cloud computing in all sectors of the economy to boost productivity. Furthermore, the EC concludes that cloud computing has the potential to slash users' IT expenditure and to enable many new services to be developed. Using the cloud, even the smallest

F. Cleary and M. Felici (Eds.): CSP Forum 2015, CCIS 530, pp. 14–25, 2015.
DOI: 10.1007/978-3-319-25360-2_2

firms can reach out to ever larger markets while governments can make their services more attractive and efficient even while reining in spending. [20].

However, besides these advantages of cloud computing, many new problems arise which are not yet sufficiently solved, especially with respect to information security and privacy [16, 21, 32]. The fundamental concept of the cloud is storage and processing by a third party (the cloud or service provider), which actually invalidates the traditional view of a perimeter in IT security. In fact, the third party becomes part of the company's own computation and storage IT infrastructure albeit not being under its full control. This situation is very problematic. Thus, economic incentives and legal tools such as service level agreements (SLAs) have been introduced to increase trust in the service provider. However, recent incidents show that these measures are by far not sufficient to guard personal data and trade secrets against illegal interceptions, insider threats, or vulnerabilities exposing data to unauthorized parties. While being processed by a provider, data is typically neither adequately protected against unauthorized read access, nor against unwanted modification, or loss of authenticity. Consequently, in the most prominent cloud deployment model today – the public cloud – the cloud service provider necessarily needs to be trusted. Security guarantees with respect to user data can only be given on a contractual basis and rest to a considerable extent on organisational (besides technical) precautions. Hence, outsourcing IT tasks to an external shared infrastructure builds upon a problematic trust model. This situation inhibits many companies in the high-assurance and high-security area to benefit from external cloud offerings: for them confidentiality, integrity, and availability are of such major importance that adequate technical measures are required—but state-of-the-art ICT can currently not provide them. Moreover, individuals using public cloud services face a considerable privacy threat too, since they typically expose more information than required to services.

1.2   Objectives

In this work we present a new approach towards cloud security which is developed by the PRISMACLOUD consortium within the EU Horizon 2020 research framework. For us, the only reasonable way to achieve the required security properties for outsourced data storage and processing is by adopting suitable cryptographic mechanisms. Thus, the vision of PRISMACLOUD is to develop the next-generation of cryptographically secured cloud services with security and privacy built in by design.

The main objectives of PRISMACLOUD are: (i) to develop next-generation cryptographically secured services for the cloud. This includes the development of novel cryptographic tools, mechanisms, and techniques ready to be used in a cloud environment to protect the security of data over its lifecycle and to protect the privacy of the users. The security shall be based on by design principles. (ii) to assess and validate the project results by fully developing and implementing three realistic use case scenarios in the areas of e-government, healthcare, and smart city services. (iii) to conduct a thorough analysis of the security of the final systems, their usability, as well as legal and information governance aspects of the new services.

The European Commission already recognised the potential future impact of cloud computing for all of us and has issued a cloud computing strategy [20]. The aim of this strategy is to protect European citizens from potential threats, while simultaneously unleashing the potential of cloud computing, for both the industry/public sector as well as for individuals. PRISMACLOUD is backing this strategy and will help to remove a major inhibitor against cloud adoption in security relevant domains by developing cloud applications, that preserve more security and privacy for citizens. It will further help to strengthen the position of European industries in the cloud domain and also strengthen European research in a field with high research competition.

1.3 EU Research Context

Ongoing research activities like SECCRIT, Cumulus, and PASSIVE[1] are extremely valuable and will be setting the standards and guidelines for secure cloud computing in the next years. However, these approaches consider the cloud infrastructure provider as being trustworthy in the sense that no information of the customers, i.e., tenants, will be leaked, nor their data will be tampered with. The cloud infrastructure provider, however, has unrestricted access to all physical and virtual resources and thus absolute control over all tenants' data and resources. The underlying assumption is, that if the cloud provider performs malicious actions against its customers, in the long run, he or she will be put out of business – if such doings are revealed. However, this assumption is very strong, especially considering the ongoing revelation of intelligence agencies' data gathering activities. Data disclosure may even be legally enforced in a way completely undetectable by the cloud provider's customers.

Through auditing and monitoring of cloud services, some of the malicious behaviour of outsiders and insiders (e.g., disgruntled employees with administrator privileges) may be detectable *ex-post*. However, that does not help a specific victim to prevent or survive such an attack. Moreover, advanced cyber-attacks directly targeting a specific victim can barely be detected and prevented with cloud auditing mechanisms or anomaly detection solutions. These methods are more efficient for the detection of large scale threats and problems and for making the infrastructure itself resilient, while keeping an acceptable level of service.

Other projects, like TClouds and PRACTICE[2] take cloud security a step further: TClouds already considers the impact of malicious provider behaviour and tries to protect users. However, it is not strongly focusing on comprehensive integration of cryptography up to the level of end-to-end security. PRACTICE, in contrast, is well aligned with our idea of secure services by means of cryptography. However, it focuses mainly on the preservation of data confidentiality for processing, when outsourced to the cloud. PRISMACLOUD is complimentary to these concepts and enhance them with cryptographic primitives for the verification of outsourced computation and other relevant functionalities to be carried

---

[1] EU-FP7: http://www.seccrit.eu/, http://www.cumulus-project.eu/, http://ict-passive.eu/.

[2] EU-FP7: http://www.tclouds-project.eu, http://www.practice-project.eu/.

out on the data in the untrusted cloud. Research activities in context of privacy in cloud computing were and are currently conducted by various projects like ABC4Trust, A4Cloud, and AU2EU[3]. PRISMACLOUD complements these efforts by further developing privacy-enhancing technologies for the use in cloud based environments.

1.4   Main Innovations

The main goal of PRISMACLOUD is to enable the deployment of highly critical data to the cloud. The required security levels for such a move shall be achieved by means of novel security enabled cloud services, pushing the boundary of cryptographic data protection in the cloud further ahead. PRISMACLOUD core innovations are presented in the following sections.

In Sect. 2.1 we outline the idea of outsourcing computations with verifiable correctness and authenticity-preservation as well as cryptographic techniques for the verification of claims about secure configurations of the virtualized cloud infrastructures. In Sect. 2.2 we discuss cryptographic data minimization and anonymization technologies. Section 2.3 outlines a distributed multi-cloud data storage architecture which shares data among several cloud providers and thus improves data security and availability. Such techniques shall avoid vendor lock-in and promote a dynamic cloud provider market, while preserving data authenticity and facilitating long-term data privacy. Additionally, we discuss cryptographic tools for a seamless integration of encryption into existing cloud services. The PRISMACLOUD work program is complemented with activities described in Sect. 3 addressing secure service composition, usability, and secure implementation and evaluation of results in pilots. In order to converge with the European Cloud Computing Strategy, a strategy for the dissemination of results into standards will also be developed within PRISMACLOUD.

2   Technical Innovations

In this section we briefly outline technical tools and concepts which summarize the technical innovations within PRISMACLOUD.

2.1   Verifiability of Data, Processing, and Infrastructure

Verifiable and Authenticity Preserving Data Processing. Verifiable computing aims at outsourcing computations to one or more untrusted processing units in a way that the result of a computation can be efficiently checked for validity. General purpose constructions for verifiable computations have made significant process over the last years [42]. There are already various implemented systems which can be deemed nearly practical, but are not yet ready for real-world

---

[3] EU-FP7: https://abc4trust.eu, http://www.a4cloud.eu, http://www.au2eu.eu.

deployment. Besides general purpose systems, there are other approaches that are optimized for specific (limited) classes of computations or particular settings, e.g., [2,14,22].

In addition to verifiability of computations, another interesting aspect is to preserve the authenticity of data that is manipulated by computations. Tools for preserving authenticity under admissible modifications are (fully) homomorphic signatures (or message authentication codes) [13]. Besides this general tool, there are signatures with more restricted capabilities, like redactable signatures introduced in [29,40], which have recently shown to offer interesting applications [26,35]. These and other functional and malleable signatures will be developed further within PRISMACLOUD to meet requirements set by cloud applications. By combining these cryptographic concepts, PRISMACLOUD aims at providing tools that allow to realize processes (with potentially various participating entities) that guarantee to preserve the authenticity and provide verifiability of involved data and computations respectively.

Integrity and Certification of Virtualized Infrastructure. The area of structural integrity and certification of virtualized infrastructures bridges between three areas: 1. attestation of component integrity, 2. security assurance of cloud topologies, and 3. graph signatures to connect these areas.

Attestation is the process in which a trusted component asserts the state of a physical or virtual component of the virtualized infrastructure, on all the layers of it. PRISMACLOUD builds upon Direct Anonymous Attestation (DAA) [9] as means to enable this assertion while preserving confidentiality and privacy. Cloud security assurance offers the analysis of cloud topologies for security properties [6–8] as well as the verifiable auditing that these properties are maintained [37]. Graph signatures [24], that is, signatures on committed graphs, are a new primitive we investigate within PRISMACLOUD, which allow two parties to engage in an interactive protocol to issue a signature on a graph. The resulting signature allows to convince a verifier that the signed graph fulfils certain security properties (e.g., isolation or connectedness) without disclosing the blueprint of the graph itself. Within PRISMACLOUD we develop and optimize the use of graph signatures for practical use in virtualized infrastructures. Their application allows an auditor to analyse the configuration of a cloud, and to issue a signature on its topology (or a sequence of signatures on dynamically changing topologies). The signature encodes the topology as a graph in a special way, such that the cloud provider can prove high-level security properties such as isolation of tenants to verifiers. Furthermore, we will bridge between cloud security assurance and verification methodology and certification. We do this by establishing a framework that issues signatures and proves security properties based on standard graph models of cloud topologies and security goals stated in formal language, such that the virtualization assurance language VALID [5].

2.2   User Privacy Protection and Usability

Privacy Preserving Service Usage. For many services in the cloud it is important that users are given means to prove their authorisation to perform or delegate a certain task. However, it is not always necessary that users reveal their full identity to the cloud, but only prove by some means that they are authorised, e.g., possess certain rights. The main obstacle in this context is that a cloud provider must still be cryptographically reassured that the user is authorised.

Attribute-based anonymous credential (ABC) systems have proven to be an important concept for privacy-preserving applications. They allow users to authenticate in an anonymous way without revealing more information than absolutely necessary to be authenticated at a service. Thus, there are strong efforts to bring them to practice[4]. Well known ABC systems are, for instance, the multi-show system Idemix [11] and the one-show system U-Prove [33]. Recently also some alternative approaches for ABC systems from malleable signature schemes [12,15] and a variant of structure-preserving signatures [27] have been proposed.

In PRISMACLOUD we aim at improving the state of the art in ABC systems and related concepts with a focus on their application in cloud computing services. Besides traditional applications such as for anonymous authentication and authorization we will also investigate their application to privacy-preserving billing [17,38] for cloud storage and computing services.

Big Data Anonymization. Anonymizing data sets is a problem which is often encountered when providing data for processing in cloud applications in a way, that a certain degree of privacy is guaranteed. However, achieving optimal k-anonymity, for instance, is known to be an NP-hard problem. Typically, researchers have focused on achieving k-anonymity with minimum data loss, thus maximizing the utility of the anonymised results. But all of these techniques assume that the dataset to be anonymised is relatively small (and fits into computer memory). In the last few years several attempts have been made to tackle the problem of anonymising large datasets.

In PRISMACLOUD, we aim to improve existing anonymisation techniques in terms of both performance and utility (minimizing information loss) for very large data sets. We strive to overcome deficiencies in current mechanisms, e.g., size limitations, speed, assumptions about quasi-identifiers, or existence of total ordering, and implement a solution suitable for very large data sets. In addition, we address issues related to distribution of very large data sets.

2.3 Securing Data (at Rest)

Confidentiality and Integrity for Unstructured Data. Protecting customer data managed in the cloud from unauthorised access by the cloud provider itself should be one of the most basic and essential functionalities of a cloud system. However, the vast majority of current cloud offerings does not provide such a functionality. One reason for this situation is that current cryptographic solutions can not be easily integrated without drastically limiting the capabilities of the storage service.

---

[4] e.g., ABC4Trust: https://abc4trust.eu/.

In PRISMACLOUD, we aim to research and develop novel secure storage solutions which are based on secret sharing and have increased flexibility. Secret sharing can also be used to provide confidentiality and integrity for data at rest with strong security guarantees in a key-less manner when working in a distributed setting. Various systems have been proposed during the last years, but most of them work in rather naive single user modes and require a trusted proxy in their setting [39]. In [4] a new type is proposed, which uses semi-active nodes to support concurrency in data storage access. It combines efficient Byzantine protocols with various types of secret sharing protocols to cope with different adversary settings in a flexible way. However, desired features such as multi-user support through the integration of a trustworthy distributed access control system or mechanisms for access privacy are still missing.

Our goal is to develop efficient and flexible secret sharing based storage solutions for dynamic environments, like the cloud, supporting different adversary models (active, passive, mixed) and multiple users. The research will focus on the design of a fully decentratlized system without single-point-of-trust and single-point-of-failure. Moreover, we will also investigate how metadata can be protected to have better access privacy.

Long-Term Security Aspects and Everlasting Privacy. To provide protection goals, such as integrity, authenticity, and confidentiality in the long-term, classic cryptographic primitives like digital signatures and encryption schemes are not sufficient. They become insecure when their security properties are defeated by advances in computer power or cryptanalytic techniques. Thus, the only approach known to address long-term confidentiality is by using proactive secret sharing, e.g., [25]. In this approach, the data is split into several shares that are stored in different locations and are renewed from time to time. Although secret sharing is needed to provide long-term confidentiality, there is no approach that allows performing publicly or privately verifiable computations or integrity preserving modifications on secret shares yet. Besides the distributed storage of data, to provide everlasting privacy (or confidentiality) for data processed in a publicly verifiable manner, the information published for auditing needs to be information-theoretically secure. Only a few solutions address this and only for specific problems, such as verifiable anonymisation of data [10] and verifiable tallying of votes, e.g., [30]. No general applicable solution is provided, nor do existing approaches show how authenticated data can be processed in a publicly verifiable way. Therefore, we aim at providing solutions for proactive secret sharing of authenticated data and techniques that allow for privately and publicly verifiable computations.

Cryptography for Seamless Service Integration. For existing applications in the cloud, it may be impossible to transparently add security features later on. Assume, for instance, encrypted data is stored in the same database table used for unencrypted data. In this case applications running on the database may be unable to use the encrypted data, causing them to crash or alternatively, to output incorrect values. Standard encryption schemes are designed for bit-strings of a fixed length and can therefore significantly alter the data format, which may cause disruptions both in storing and using the data.

To address this problem, techniques like format-preserving encryption (FPE), order-preserving encryption (OPE), and tokenizaiton have emerged as most useful tools. In FPE schemes the encrypted ciphertexts have the same format as the messages, i.e. they can be directly applied without adapting the application itself. OPE schemes, on the other hand, maintain the order between messages in the original domain, thus allowing execution of range queries on encrypted data.

In PRISMACLOUD we aim to address the shortcomings of the existing FPE and OPE schemes. It can be shown that existing FPE schemes for general formats, e.g., name, address, etc., are inefficient, lack in their security level, and do not provide a clear way for format definition, thus making them practically unusable. We propose to address both issues (security and efficiency) and develop an FPE scheme for general formats that: (i) is more efficient; (ii) provides an acceptable security guarantee; (iii) supports a complex format definition; (iv) could be employed to solve practical problems, e.g., data sharing for clusters of private clouds. For OPE we aim to further progress the state of the art from both security and performance perspectives.

3   Methodology, Guidelines, and Evaluation

In this section we discuss how our technical innovations will be put to practice and how user's trust in these solutions will be improved.

3.1   Holistic Security Models

We have previously described many cryptographically strong building blocks. However, combining the building blocks of PRISMACLOUD correctly would require the developers to have a solid understanding of their cryptographic strength. The approach of service orientation [19] has increasingly been adopted as one of the main paradigms for developing complex distributed systems out of re-usable components called services. PRISMACLOUD aims to use the potential benefits of this software engineering approach, but not build yet another semi-automated or automated technique for service composition. To compose these building blocks into secure higher level services without an in-depth understanding of their cryptographic underpinnings PRISMACLOUD will identify which existing models for the security of compositions are adequate to deal with the complexity and heterogeneity.

PRISMACLOUD will adopt working and established solutions and assumes that the working way of composing services can be a way to allow secure composition. When each service can be described using standard description languages this allows extending composition languages [3] to provide further capabilities, e.g., orchestrations, security, and transactions, to service-oriented solutions [34]. In PRISMACLOUD we want to reduce the complexity further, just like recently, mashups [18] of web APIs provided means for non-experts to define simple work-flows. Within PRISMACLOUD we will develop a description of not only the functionality of each cryptographic building block but also of their limitations and composability.

3.2 Usability Concepts and End-User Aspects

Cryptographic tools, such as secret sharing, verifiable computation, or anonymous credentials, are fundamental technologies for secure cloud services and to preserve end users' privacy by enforcing data minimization. End users are still unfamiliar with such cryptographic concepts that are counterintuitive to them and for which no obvious real-world analogies exist. In previous HCI studies it has been shown that users have therefore difficulties to develop the correct mental models for data minimisation techniques such as anonymous credentials [43] or the new German identity card [28]. Moreover, end users often do not trust the claim that such privacy-enhancing technologies will really protect their privacy [1]. Similarly, users may not trust claims of authenticity and verifiability functionality of malleable and of functional signature schemes. In our earlier research work, we have explored different ways in which comprehensive mental models of the data minimization property of anonymous credentials can be evoked on end users [43]. PRISMACLOUD extends this work by conducting research on suitable metaphors for evoking correct mental models for other privacy-enhancing protocols and cryptographic schemes used in PRISMACLOUD. Besides, it researches what social trust factors can establish trust in PRISMACLOUD technology and how this can be matched into the user interfaces.

Moreover, previous studies have shown the vulnerability of information and communication technology systems, and especially also of cloud systems, to illegal and criminal activities [23]. We will take a critical appraisal of the secure cloud systems proposed in PRISMACLOUD and will analyze, whether they live up to the security promises in practical applications. We will give an indication for individuals, and for corporate and institutional security managers, what it means in practice to entrust sensitive data in specific use cases to systems claiming to implement, e.g., "everlasting privacy" [31]. Besides licit use, we will assess the impact of potential criminal uses and misuses of the secure cloud infrastructures to foster, enhance, and promote cybercrime. We want to anticipate threats resulting from misuse, deception, hijacking, or misappropriation by licit entities.

3.3 Demonstration and Evaluation

As feasibility proof, three use cases from the fields of smart city, E-Government, and E-Health will be augmented with the PRISMACLOUD tools in accordance with the elaborated methodologies and evaluated by the project participants.

In the *Smart City* domain, the privacy tools will be used to augment a prototype of the European disabled batch implementation[5] with data minimization technologies. Furthermore, an end-to-end secure information sharing system will

---

[5] EU-FP7 SIMON Project: http://www.simon-project.eu.

help to protect confidentiality, integrity, and availability of surveillance data of public areas for law enforcement units. In the *E-Government* domain, we will develop a secure community cloud approach, where governmental IT service providers are able to pool their resources for increased availability and business continuity. In a semi-trusted model every provider shares parts of its storage infrastructure with other providers in a verifiable manner but without breaking confidentiality of data. In addition, it hosts some business support services in an authentic way. The protection of integrity and authenticity of health data will be demonstrated in the *E-Health* scenario, where telemedicine data will be secured throughout their whole life-cycle in the cloud with increased agility. The data will be even processed in a verifiable manner to avoid tampering of third parties with sensitive personal information.

4   Conclusion and Outlook

According to the importance of the project goals, i.e. to enable secure dependable cloud solutions, PRISMACLOUD will have a significant impact in many areas. On a European level, PRISMACLOUD's disruptive potential of results lies in its provision of a basis for the actual implementation and deployment of security enabled cloud services. Jointly developed by European scientists and industrial experts, the technology can act as an enabling technology in many sectors, like health care, electronic government, and smart cities. Increasing adoption of cloud services, with all its positive impact on productivity, and creation of jobs may be stimulated. On a societal level, PRISMACLOUD potentially removes a major roadblock towards the adoption of efficient cloud solutions to a potential benefit of the end-users. Through the use of privacy-preserving data minimization functionalities, and depersonalization features, the amount of data being collected about end-users may effectively be reduced, maintaining the full functionality of the services. We will explicitly analyse potential negative consequences and potential misuses (cybercrime) of secure cloud services. Additionally, the potential impact for European industry is huge: PRISMACLOUD results may contribute to pull some of the cloud business currently concentrated elsewhere to Europe and create sustainable business opportunities for companies in Europe. Equally important is the potential impact of PRISMACLOUD for the European scientific community, as its results will be very much on the edge of scientific research.

Acknowledgements. This work has received funding from the European Union's Horizon 2020 research and innovation programme under grant agreement No 644962.

References

1. Andersson, C., Camenisch, J., Crane, S., Fischer-Hübner, S., Leenes, R., Pearson, S., Pettersson, J.S., Sommer, D.: Trust in PRIME. In: ISSPIT, pp. 552–559 (2005)
2. Backes, M., Fiore, D., Reischuk, R.M.: Verifiable delegation of computation on outsourced data. In: ACM CCS, pp. 863–874. ACM (2013)

3. Beek, M.T., Bucchiarone, A., Gnesi, S.: A Survey on Service Composition Approaches: From Industrial Standards to Formal Methods. Technical report 2006-TR-15 (2006)
4. Bessani, A., Correia, M., Quaresma, B., André, F., Sousa, P.: Depsky: dependable and secure storage in a cloud-of-clouds. Trans. Storage **9**(4), 1–12 (2013)
5. Bleikertz, S., Groß, T.: A virtualization assurance language for isolation and deployment. In: POLICY. IEEE, June 2011
6. Bleikertz, S., Groß, T., Mödersheim, S.: Security analysis of dynamic infrastructure clouds (extended abstract), September 2013
7. Bleikertz, S., Groß, T., Schunter, M., Eriksson, K.: Automated information flow analysis of virtualized infrastructures. In: Atluri, V., Diaz, C. (eds.) ESORICS 2011. LNCS, vol. 6879, pp. 392–415. Springer, Heidelberg (2011)
8. Bleikertz, S., Vogel, C., Groß, T.: Cloud radar: near real-time detection of security failures in dynamic virtualized infrastructures. In: ACSAC, pp. 26–35. ACM (2014)
9. Brickell, E., Camenisch, J., Chen, L.: Direct anonymous attestation. In: ACM CCS, pp. 225–234. ACM Press (2004)
10. Buchmann, J., Demirel, D., van de Graaf, J.: Towards a publicly-verifiable mix-net providing everlasting privacy. In: Financial Cryptography, pp. 197–204 (2013)
11. Camenisch, J., Herreweghen, E.V.: Design and implementation of the idemix anonymous credential system. In: ACM CCS, pp. 21–30. ACM (2002)
12. Canard, S., Lescuyer, R.: Protecting privacy by sanitizing personal data: a new approach to anonymous credentials. In: ASIA CCS, pp. 381–392. ACM (2013)
13. Catalano, D.: Homomorphic signatures and message authentication codes. In: Abdalla, M., De Prisco, R. (eds.) SCN 2014. LNCS, vol. 8642, pp. 514–519. Springer, Heidelberg (2014)
14. Catalano, D., Marcedone, A., Puglisi, O.: Authenticating computation on groups: new homomorphic primitives and applications. In: Sarkar, P., Iwata, T. (eds.) ASIACRYPT 2014, Part II. LNCS, vol. 8874, pp. 193–212. Springer, Heidelberg (2014)
15. Chase, M., Kohlweiss, M., Lysyanskaya, A., Meiklejohn, S.: Malleable signatures: new definitions and delegatable anonymous credentials. In: CSF, pp. 199–213. IEEE (2014)
16. Cloud Security Alliance: Cloud security alliance website (2009). https://cloudsecurityalliance.org. Accessed 31 March 2015
17. Danezis, G., Kohlweiss, M., Rial, A.: Differentially private billing with rebates. In: Filler, T., Pevný, T., Craver, S., Ker, A. (eds.) IH 2011. LNCS, vol. 6958, pp. 148–162. Springer, Heidelberg (2011)
18. Di Lorenzo, G., Hacid, H., Benatallah, B., Paik, H.Y.: Data integration in mashups. Sigmod Rec. **38**(1), 59–66 (2009)
19. Erl, T.: Service-Oriented Architecture: Concepts, Technology, and Design. Pearson Education India, Delhi (2006)
20. European Commission: European cloud computing strategy "unleashing the potential of cloud computing in europe" (2012). http://ec.europa.eu/digital-agenda/en/european-cloud-computing-strategy. Accessed 31 March 2015
21. European Union Agency for Network and Information Security-ENISA: Cloud computing repository. http://www.enisa.europa.eu/activities/Resilience-and-CIIP/cloud-computing
22. Fiore, D., Gennaro, R., Pastro, V.: Efficiently verifiable computation on encrypted data. In: ACM CCS, pp. 844–855 (2014)
23. Ghernaouti-Helie, S.: Cyber Power - Crime. Conflict and Security in Cyberspace. EPFL Press, Burlington (2013)

24. Groß, T.: Signatures and efficient proofs on committed graphs and NP-statements. In: Böhme, R., Okamoto, T. (eds.) FC 2015. LNCS, vol. 8975, pp. 293–314. Springer, Heidelberg (2015)
25. Gupta, V.H., Gopinath, K.: G_{its}^2 vsr: an information theoretical secure verifiable secret redistribution protocol for long-term archival storage. In: Security in Storage Workshop, SISW 2007, pp. 22–33. IEEE Computer Society, Washington, DC, USA (2007). http://dx.doi.org/10.1109/SISW.2007.9
26. Hanser, C., Slamanig, D.: Blank digital signatures. In: ASIA CCS. ACM (2013)
27. Hanser, C., Slamanig, D.: Structure-preserving signatures on equivalence classes and their application to anonymous credentials. In: Sarkar, P., Iwata, T. (eds.) ASIACRYPT 2014. LNCS, vol. 8873, pp. 491–511. Springer, Heidelberg (2014)
28. Harbach, M., Fahl, S., Rieger, M., Smith, M.: On the acceptance of privacy-preserving authentication technology: the curious case of national identity cards. In: De Cristofaro, E., Wright, M. (eds.) PETS 2013. LNCS, vol. 7981, pp. 245–264. Springer, Heidelberg (2013)
29. Johnson, R., Molnar, D., Song, D., Wagner, D.: Homomorphic signature schemes. In: Preneel, B. (ed.) CT-RSA 2002. LNCS, vol. 2271, pp. 244–262. Springer, Heidelberg (2002)
30. Moran, T., Naor, M.: Split-ballot voting: everlasting privacy with distributed trust. ACM Trans. Inf. Syst. Secur. **13**(2), 246–255 (2010)
31. Müller-Quade, J., Unruh, D.: Long-term security and universal composability. J. Cryptol. **23**(4), 594–671 (2010)
32. National Institute of Standards and Technology-NIST: Cloud computing program. http://www.nist.gov/itl/cloud/index.cfm. Accessed 31 March 2015
33. Paquin, C., Zaverucha, G.: U-prove cryptographic specification v1.1, revision 3. Technical report, Microsoft Corporation (2013)
34. Pfeffer, H., Linner, D., Steglich, S.: Modeling and controlling dynamic service compositions. In: Computing in the Global Information Technology, pp. 210–216. IEEE (2008)
35. Pöhls, H.C., Samelin, K.: On updatable redactable signatures. In: Boureanu, I., Owesarski, P., Vaudenay, S. (eds.) ACNS 2014. LNCS, vol. 8479, pp. 457–475. Springer, Heidelberg (2014)
36. PRWeb: A cloud computing forecast summary for 2013–2017 from idc, gartner and kpmg, citing a study by accenture (2013). http://www.prweb.com/releases/2013/11/prweb11341594.htm. Accessed 31 March 2015
37. Schiffman, J., Sun, Y., Vijayakumar, H., Jaeger, T.: Cloud verifier: verifiable auditing service for IaaS clouds. In: CSA, June 2013
38. Slamanig, D.: Efficient schemes for anonymous yet authorized and bounded use of cloud resources. In: Miri, A., Vaudenay, S. (eds.) SAC 2011. LNCS, vol. 7118, pp. 73–91. Springer, Heidelberg (2012)
39. Slamanig, D., Hanser, C.: On cloud storage and the cloud of clouds approach. In: ICITST-2012, pp. 649–655. IEEE Press (2012)
40. Steinfeld, R., Bull, L., Zheng, Y.: Content extraction signatures. In: Kim, K. (ed.) ICISC 2001. LNCS, vol. 2288, p. 285. Springer, Heidelberg (2002)
41. Transparency Market Research: Cloud computing services market - global industry size, share, trends, analysis and forecasts 2012–2018 (2012). http://www.transparencymarketresearch.com/cloud-computing-services-market.html. Accessed 31 March 2015
42. Walfish, M., Blumberg, A.J.: Verifying computations without reexecuting them. Commun. ACM **58**(2), 74–84 (2015)
43. Wästlund, E., Angulo, J., Fischer-Hübner, S.: Evoking comprehensive mental models of anonymous credentials. In: iNetSeC, pp. 1–14 (2011)

Privacy Aware Access Control for Cloud-Based Data Platforms

Dónal McCarthy[1][✉], Paul Malone[1], Johannes Hange[2], Kenny Doyle[1],
Eric Robson[1], Dylan Conway[1], Stepan Ivanov[1], Lukasz Radziwonowicz[2],
Robert Kleinfeld[2], Theodoros Michalareas[3], Timotheos Kastrinogiannis[3],
Nikos Stasinos[3], and Fenareti Lampathaki[4]

[1] Telecommunications Software and Sytems Group,
Waterford Institute of Technology, Waterford, Ireland
{dmccarthy,pmalone}@tssg.org
[2] Fraunhofer - Institut für Offene Kommunikationssysteme FOKUS, Berlin, Germany
[3] VELTI SA, Athens, Greece
[4] National Technical University of Athens, Athens, Greece

Abstract. This paper presents OPENi's Personal Cloudlets framework
as a novel approach to enhancing users access control and privacy over
their persinal data on a cloud-based platform. This paper describes the
OPENi concepts and the requirements that influenced the design and
implementation of OPENi's Personal Cloudlet Framework. We describe
the architecture and how OPENi, through the use of REST based endpoints, object-based access control, OPENi Types, and stateless JSON
Web Token (JWT), allows users share, reuse, and control access to their
data across many mobile applications while maintaining cloud scalability. This paper also describes how a number of the Personal Cloudlet
framework's features enhance a users privacy and control. These features
include the User Dashboard, the Privacy Preserving Data Aggregator,
and the fine grained access control mechanism.

Keywords: Personal data · Privacy · Fine-grained access control ·
Privacy-preserving data aggregator

1 Introduction

In recent years the focal point of the digital economy is that of personal information. Internet companies such as Google and Facebook utilise a business model
of analysing user data in order to accurately facilitate the targeting of advertise-
ments, and the influencing of behaviour. The smartphone and tablet application
market have also adopted this business model. The privacy policies of these services generally operate on a "take it or leave it" basis, where users can either
reject this gathering of personal information and not using a service or application, or they agree to this information gathering and use the service under terms
and conditions which they have little control over. The emerging move towards

© Springer International Publishing Switzerland 2015
F. Cleary and M. Felici (Eds.): CSP Forum 2015, CCIS 530, pp. 26–37, 2015.
DOI: 10.1007/978-3-319-25360-2_3

increased use of cloud computing compounds these trends as more user data will be stored at remote locations.

OPENi [7] provides a platform which enables users with control over their personal data. The main components of this platform are the API framework and the Personal Cloudlet framework. The API framework allows for interoperability between cloud based services, and the Personal Cloudlet framework is a virtual space that securely stores user data and gives users primary control over that data. OPENi allows for users to decide which elements of their personal data they are prepared to share by providing the option of fine grained access control. The OPENi platform addresses many of the problems raised by the emerging business models, by empowering the user to take control of their digital identity and personal data.

In this paper we describe the privacy requirements for the Personal Cloudlet concept, its specification, and its open source implementation.

2   Background

2.1   The OPENi Project

OPENi's aims are to inspire innovation in the European mobile applications industry by improving the interoperability of cloud-based services and trust in personal cloud storage. It achieves this through the development of a user-centric, open source mobile cloud applications data platform [8].

The platform incorporates an open framework that is capable of interoperating with many cloud-based services, abstracting the integration challenges to a single open standard without losing service features. It is a single platform that inherently promotes innovation by offering application developers an advanced framework in which to design and build complex applications involving the combination of independent cloud-based services.

A central concept of OPENi is to reduce the fragmentation and duplication of citizens' data. OPENi provides mobile application end-users with a single location to store and control their personal data. This Personal Cloudlet enables consumers to manage what information is available to each application. The cloudlet thus becomes a single authoritative source for users' personal data and content. Consumers are therefore assured that their data is not being used without their consent.

The combination of the open API and Personal Cloudlet concept creates a single platform of user data and service connectivity making OPENi a very powerful and beneficial platform for consumers, application developers, and service providers.

2.2   The OPENi Architecture

The OPENi platform is composed of four distinct but interrelated frameworks which are shown in Fig. 1. Each component is developed using whatever languages and application stack best suited their functionality, yet all are presented

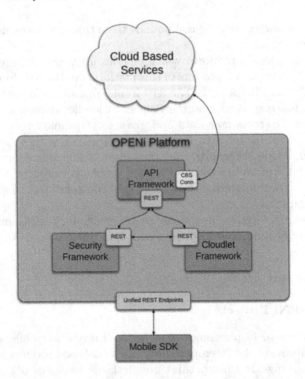

Fig. 1. OPENi platform's high level architecture. The diagram presents the four major components that comprise the platform: (1) the mobile client library, (2) the security framework, (3) the API framework, and (4) the Cloudlet framework.

to the mobile developers through a single unified suite of REST Endpoints. Internally, the individual frameworks also interact with each other through their respective REST endpoints and SDKs. All interaction with external cloud-based services is performed by the API framework through its Cloud-based services (CBS) connectors. The platform components are described below:

Mobile Client Library. To provide convenient access to the API, security, and Personal Cloudlet frameworks, OPENi provides a two mobile client libraries. The first is a cross platform HTML/Javascript library for use in HTML5 and Apache Cordova [1] mobile web-apps. The second is a native Android client library. The libraries abstract and simplify access to OPENi services across multiple mobile platforms and are designed to promote rapid application development for easy developer on-boarding. In simple terms it aggregates the REST clients of the three frameworks and also includes a significant number of enhancements including a number of security mechanisms and UI components.

Security Framework. The security framework provides access control functionality which is tightly coupled with the Cloudlet Framework and provides users with more control over their personal data and the cloud-based services that they interact with.

API Framework. The OPENi Graph API Framework [12,16] is an open framework that is capable of interoperating with a variety of cloud-based services, abstracting the integration challenges to a single open standard without sacrificing service features. It promotes innovation by offering application developers an advanced framework that will enable them to design and build complex applications involving the combinations of independent cloud-based services.

Personal Cloudlet Framework. The OPENi Personal Cloudlet framework [10,13,14] provides application consumers with a single location to store and control their personal data. The Personal Cloudlet, in conjunction with the security framework, empowers application consumers to remain in control of their data. The remainder of this paper focuses on the objectives, concept and implementation of the Personal Cloudlet framework.

2.3   OPENi Cloudlet Objectives

Among the objectives of the OPENi project[1] the following apply to the Personal Cloudlet Framework:

1. To build key technological enablers to ensure the practical applicability and efficient use of the OPENi APIs such as: a web based security and authorisation framework that will satisfy the service provider's requirements and a context broker that will enable the sharing of context information between applications in accordance with the users privacy settings.
2. To deliver an open source platform that will allow application consumers to create, deploy and manage their personal space in the cloud (Personal Cloudlet). Each Personal Cloudlet will constitute a novel entity that will be linked to its user's identity over the web in a similar way that a social profile does today.
3. To provide and promote a novel, user-centric application experience of cloud-based services not only across different devices but also inherently across different applications. The OPENi framework will enable application consumers to share and distribute their data across their applications.
4. To ensure the OPENi platform maintains a low barrier to entry for application developers and service providers.

2.4   Security Analysis

OPENi deliverable D2.3 [11] gives a security analysis addressing specific security and privacy facets of the OPENi solution as a whole as well as its individual components. A comprehensive privacy and security analysis is beyond the scope of this paper and the reader is recommended to read deliverable D2.3 for a comprehensive analysis. Here we will discuss only the privacy considerations relevant to the Cloudlet and API frameworks.

---

[1] OPENi Objectives, http://www.openi-ict.eu/objectives/.

2.5 Privacy for OPENi API and Personal Cloudlet Frameworks

In general terms, privacy consists of restricting access to information only to a limited set of entities for whom access is permitted. In the OPENi platform, applications developed using the API framework can request access to information about users stored in the Cloudlet platform. For instance, an advertising application may use information from a specific user account to identify a list of potential preferred products. End-users must however maintain the right to decide which entities have access to which information in their personal cloudlet. High-level software privacy mechanisms have to be implemented in order to enable end users to manage this access to their data. Delverable D2.3 [11] discusses these privacy considerations across the data security lifecycle through the functions of *Access*, *Process* and *Store* in conjunction with actors and locations [15].

The OPENi Cloudlet platform must enable users to manage access control over their personal cloudlets. This means that higher-level software controls have to be implemented. These controls are categorised as follows:

- Digital Identities
- Authentication
- Authorisation
- Delegation
- Auditing
- Accounting
- Access Control
- Identity Federation
- Single Sign-On (SSO)

One of the main challenges of access management over clouds is the lack of central governance and identity information architecture. This distributed environment complicates orchestrated interactions over sensitive data. By implementing Identity and Access Management the OPENi Cloudlet platform solves access for distributed and changing user populations with persistence, consistence and efficiency.

3 Personal Cloudlet Framework Implementation

This section contains a description of the implementation of the Personal Cloudlet.

3.1 Personal Cloudlet Framework Architecture

The Personal Cloudlet framework is a multi-tenancy web service with a single datastore that also supports off platform data storage. Internally the Cloudlet Framework is designed and implemented as a distributed application based on the micro-services paradigm. A micro-services architecture was chosen because it supports functional separation, heterogeneity, resilience, scalability, load balancing and economy.

3.2   Technology Selection

The software stack selected to implement the Personal Cloudlet Framework is influenced by the decision to follow a micro-services architecture approach. The stack includes: ZeroMQ [9] as the messaging library, JavaScript and Node.js as the programming language and runtime, CouchBase [2] as the datastore, Mongrel2 [6] as the webserver, and Docker [3] as the cloud deployment platform.

For details on our decision to implement the Personal Cloudlet Framework as a distributed applications and the technologies choices that were taken to realise this, please refer to OPENi deliverable D3.5 Cloudlet Platform Design [14].

3.3   Framework Components

Figure 2 shows the components that together form the Personal Cloudlet Framework. In many cases, these components map directly to a standalone worker, others are cross component but logically separated.

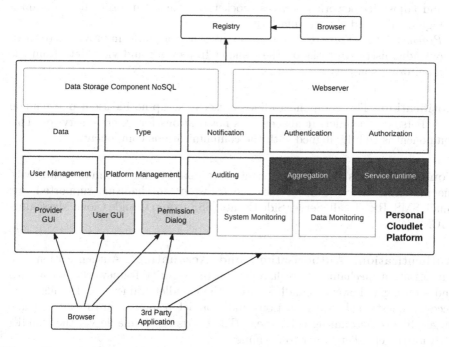

Fig. 2. The personal Cloudlet framework is composed of the following standalone components. Components shaded in light grey are external facing user interfaces, dark grey shaded components signify non-core service enabler components.

Data Storage Component. A data storage component capable of storing user, application and internal cloudlet data. This data can be in various formats such as text, graphical, audio, video etc. The data storage component of the cloudlet framework is therefore capable of accommodating binary files as well as structured JSON data.

Platform Management. The platform management components will be responsible for managing the underlying resources, which serve the cloudlet framework. These components are available only to the platform provider. The following components are available:

- *System Monitoring* - For infrastructure metrics, a Round Robin Database (RRD) tool is integrated directly into the application. Key endpoint actions are monitored and logged, including creating cloudlets, inserting data and querying cloudlet data stores. This component provides comprehensive information of the platform as a whole and provides better platform management.
- *Orchestration* - This feature enables the platform providers to add, remove and adjust framework resources (docker containers) in order to maintain a high quality and efficient platform.
- *Provider GUI* - This GUI serves as an interface for platform providers to carry out administrative tasks on the cloudlet framework and view data from the monitoring component.

Notification. This component allows a user to setup notifications of events on their Personal Cloudlet. It also enables notifications for external services. This component is tightly aligned with the communications component.

Communications. This component is responsible for communicating with the platforms users. Current message transport mechanisms supported are: email, SMS, REST call, Server Side Events (SSEs), and Google Cloud Messaging-(GCM) [4].

Authentication, Authorisation, and Accounting. Authentication and authorisation mechanisms are handled by the security framework. Accounting and auditing is however handled within the cloudlet framework. Details of all access requests, subsequent actions and cloudlet responses are monitored and logged by the accounting component. These logs are available via the cloudlet GUI for the cloudlet owner to examine.

Data Access. All data that exists in a cloudlet will be accessed via the Data API and the Type API. They ensure a consistent access point for all services such as applications, the API framework, and 3rd party services. In conjunction with the Authentication, Authorisation, Accounting component and permissions, the cloudlet owner is in full control of who and what can access each piece of data in their Personal Cloudlet.

Cloudlet GUIs. To empower Cloudlet owners in the management of their cloudlets they have a standalone GUI, separate to the mobile application interface. GUI features include data deletion, access logs viewing, preference editing and permissions editing.

Data Aggregator. The data aggregation component will offer third parties the ability to view aggregated user data from multiple cloudlets while concealing the individual cloudlet owner's identity. More details on this component is described later in this paper.

3.4   User-Centric & Privacy-Preserving Features

This section outlines the key privacy preserving and user empowering features of the Personal Cloudlet Framework which enable the user to attain more control over their data than tradition data platforms.

Session and Authorisation Tokens. On the Cloudlet Framework, tokens are used to apply a context to 3rd party access to Personal Cloudlets and enable data masking accordingly using an OAuth 2.0 compliant workflow. When app developers register an app on the framework a client key and secret key is generated for them. Both these keys are required to initialise the OPENi client side library. Any time the app user interacts with the server side OAuth HTML views theses keys are passed to give the interaction app context. The two primary OAuth views are the login dialog and the permissions dialogs. In the case of the login view, the user must provide their OPENi credentials to log into their Personal Cloudlets. If the user credentials are valid and the application's client and secret key are valid, the system generates a token with the user identifier and the application identifier embedded in it. This token is then passed to the client side library where is it embedded as a HTTP header in all other interaction with the Personal Cloudlet framework. These tokens are integral to maintaining the framework's statelessness and play a role in attaining web-scalablity. OPENi extends JSON Web Tokens (JWT)[5] to include this functionality. JWTs are digitally signed base64 encoded JSON objects that enable stateless REST based frameworks manage sessions and claims.

Data Reusability; App Interoperability. All Personal Cloudlet data is persisted to a NoSQL Document store. Accordingly a user's Personal Cloudlet is composed of a number of JSON Objects. As the system is designed to enable a user to share their data across multiple applications and services OPENi implemented a mechanism that exposes the structure of Personal Cloudlet Objects without revealing the objects content. In essence all Objects (user data) created on the Cloudlet Framework must adhere to a predefined OPENi Type. A Type is comparable to an SQL schema in that it defines strict parameters on against which data structures are validated before they are persisted to a

Personal Cloudlet. Like a schema, the Type sets strict criteria about an Object's construction including its datapoints: name, its primitive type (int, boolean, string, data, etc.), whether the datapoint is required, and an optional enumeration of accepted values. OPENi Types are allowed to specify other OPENi Types within them for more advanced use-cases. For convenience we provide an OPENi Type builder on the platform.

On the Personal Cloudlet framework, all Types are public and app developers are free to reuse Types created by others. Through a registry, developers can query how much a Type is used on the platform. Types are indexed and searchable both by number of objects of that Type and of amount of Cloudlets using that Type. However, to preserve privacy we do not indicate which Personal Cloudlets have objects of a particular Type. A third party service provider has the choice to reuse an existing type or create a custom type of their own. App developers cannot prevent another service provider reusing that type as it belongs to the end users as a collective. These OPENi Types and the associated registry facilitate data re-use and interoperability between devices, applications, and service providers.

Fine Grained Access Control. The Personal Cloudlet framework manages Cloudlet data access by attaching permissions objects to each individual Cloudlet Object. The permissions objects list the apps that are allowed to create, read, update and delete the object as well as specifying which app actually created the Object. An app developer can request access to data on a user's Personal Cloudlet on a per Type or per Object basis. Also the app developer can scope their permission request to Objects of a Type created by that app or by Objects of a Type across the users Cloudlet i.e. Cloudlet Objects created by other services.

While the permissions data is embedded within the Object it is not placed there through the Object APIs, instead it is through a separate permissions mechanism with its own API. In a similar fashion to which the developer keys are embedded in the mobile application, the developer must include their permissions requests in a manifest which is published on the platform. When a user logs into their Personal Cloudlet for the first time with the app, the client side library send the permissions manifest to a server-side HTML page which parses it and presents the permissions request to the end user in a user-friendly manner where they have the option to agree or disagree. In some cases the user is able to modify the scope of access and expect the app to still work i.e. change it from Cloudlet scope to app scope. Once a user agrees to the permissions, they are persisted to the framework through the Permission API. When they are sent they are accompanied with a JWT containing the user and developer/app context, this context enables the system to verify the actors and perform the CRUD updates accordingly. The Personal Cloudlet owner can edit their permissions and update access to individual objects through the user portal at any time.

Persisting the permissions with the data has ramifications for a number of actions, create and update actions requires a read and write datastore operation, whereas read and delete operations only require a single database read action. There are also transactional implications for updates to existing permissions. OPENi uses an eventual consistency model for propagating permission changes to existing objects. While the client side is informed immediately that the permissions have persisted, a separate worker on the system finds Cloudlet Objects that have to be updated and changes their CRUD entries. When the worker has completed the work for that permission update it changes the status of the permissions object and sends a notification to the mobile client.

Mobile Client Library. The Personal Cloudlet Client library incorporates a number of privacy preserving features, some of which have already been listed. The SDK also ensures that all data is securely transported to the Personal Cloudlet Framework. For added security it also give the Cloudlet owner the option to encrypt their data on their client.

User Dashboard. The user dashboard is an off-application HTML dashboard that the user can visit. It allows the user to view their Personal Cloudlet from their own context, i.e. as the owner. It allows them to browse all the data within their Cloudlet, view access request logs, and view or edit app permissions outside of the applications. The main features of the User Dashboard are:

- *Data browsing* - the Personal Cloudlet owner can view their data categorised by type, app, or temporally. It enables them to view data in their Cloudlet from each of their 3rd party apps perspective.
- *Auditing* - The user can view their Personal Cloudlets access request logs, categorised by allowed and denied request and by 3rd party. The logs can be viewed in table format or through the Piwik analytics engine. With Piwik we reversed the traditional paradigm of analytics engines. Normally analytics engines present a users interaction with a service to the service provider, with OPENi we do the opposite by presenting analytics based on service providers interaction with the user's Personal Cloudlet.
- *Permissions* - the user can view and edit all permissions associated with their app. They can do this to current and historical permissions.
- *Privacy feedback* - a user friendly privacy feedback mechanism which analyses a users Cloudlet and permissions settings and presents simplified feedback and guidelines regarding their data leakage.
- *Notifications* - allows user setup notifications attached to their Personal Cloudlet so that they are informed of access requests and permission requests on their cloudlet.

A link to the user dashboard is embedded in the OPENi client library settings UI component, it opens in the mobile devices mobile application, the reason why the user dashboard isn't embedded in the SDK is to prevent phishing.

Privacy Preserving Data Aggregator. The privacy preserving data aggregation (DA) component offers 3rd-party services that integrate with the Personal Cloudlet framework, the ability to view aggregated user data from across multiple cloudlets while concealing the individual cloudlet owner's identity. The Personal Cloudlet owner has to explicitly opt-in to the data aggregator for each service. When the Cloudlet framework gets a request for aggregated data it negotiates with the permissions component to identify cloudlets that wish to share data with the 3rd party. It then pulls the data from each cloudlet, aggregates it, analyses it for privacy leakage and sends the results to the 3rd party.

The purpose of the DA is to allow e-commerce business models that depend heavily on analytics, to migrate to the Personal Cloudlet framework and operate as before but in a more open and privacy preserving way. Each deployment of the OPENi platform will have a separate, independent data aggregation component. This component does not aim to integrate with the corresponding component on other OPENi Cloudlet Platforms.

3.5   Open Source Project - PEAT

The platform is released as open source software via github as the PEAT platform[2]. The github repository includes a set of deploy scripts to build and run the platform as well as android code examples to get started with the platform.

4   Conclusion and Next Steps

This paper has described how the OPENi project implements fine grained access control to empower users with control over how applications can use their data. This is achieved through the use of REST based endpoints, object-based access control, OPENi Types, and stateless JSON Web Tokens (JWT). The implementation allows users to share, reuse, and control access to their data across many mobile applications while maintaining cloud scalability.

The open source OPENi implementation is being leveraged by a number of commercialisation projects, funded by Enterprise Ireland, for development of scalable cloud based mobile applications enriched with the privacy preserving access control mechanisms.

Work currently under way with the OPENi project includes the validation of the implementation. This validation work will be reported in follow up publications.

Acknowledgment. The research and subsequent implementation reported in this paper has been funded by the European Community's Seventh Framework Programme (FP7) under grant agreement FP7-ICT-317883.

---

[2] PEAT - Personal Data, Apis, and Trust, http://www.peat-platform.org/.

References

1. Apache Cordova. http://cordova.apache.org/. Accessed 15 October 2015
2. Couchbase Server. http://www.couchbase.com/. Accessed 15 January 2015
3. Docker: Build, Ship and Run Any App, Anywhere. https://www.docker.com/. Accessed 15 January 2015
4. Google Cloud Messaging for Android. https://developer.android.com/google/gcm/index.html. Accessed 15 January 2015
5. JSON Web Token (JWT). http://jwt.io/. Accessed 15 January 2015
6. Mongrel2. http://mongrel2.org/. Accessed 15 January 2015
7. OPENi - Open-Source, Web-Based, Framework for Integrating Applications with Cloud-based Services and Personal Cloudlets. http://www.openi-ict.eu/. Accessed 15 January 2015
8. OPENi open source project. https://github.com/OPENi-ict/. Accessed 15 January 2015
9. ZeroMQ. http://zeromq.org/. Accessed 15 January 2015
10. Doyle, K., McCarthy, D.: OPENi White Paper: An End Users Perspective: Digital Identity Putting the Genie Back in the Bottle, September 2014. http://www.openi-ict.eu/wp-content/uploads/2014/07/openi_whitepaper.pdf. Accessed 15 January 2015
11. Illera, R., Ortega, S., Petychakis, M.: OPENi Deliverable D2.3: Security and Privacy Considerations for Cloud-based Services and Cloudlets, January 2013. http://www.openi-ict.eu/wp-content/uploads/2013/11/OPENi_D2.3.pdf. Accessed 15 January 2015
12. Iosif, A., et al.: A community-based, graph API framework to integrate and orchestrate cloud-based services. In: Proceedings of AICCSA. IEEE Computer Society (2014), awaiting publication
13. Kleinfeld, R., et al.: OPENi Deliverable D3.6: OPENi Security and Privacy Specification, September 2014. http://www.openi-ict.eu/wp-content/uploads/2014/10/OPENi_D3.6.pdf. Accessed 15 January 2015
14. McCarthy, D., et al.: OPENi Deliverable D3.5: OPENi Cloudlet Framework Design Document, September 2014. http://www.openi-ict.eu/wp-content/uploads/2014/10/OPENi_D3.5.pdf. Accessed 15 January 2015
15. Mogul, R.: Data Security Lifecycle 2.0, September 2014. https://www.securosis.com/blog/data-security-lifecycle-2.0. Accessed 15 January 2015
16. Biliri, E., Tsouroplis, R., Lampathaki, F., Askounis, D., Petychakis, M., Alvertis, I.: Enterprise collaboration framework for managing, advancing and unifying the functionality of multiple cloud-based services with the help of a graph API. In: Camarinha-Matos, L.M., Afsarmanesh, H. (eds.) Collaborative Systems for Smart Networked Environments. IFIP AICT, vol. 434, pp. 153–160. Springer, Heidelberg (2014)

Security and Privacy Technologies

Real-World Post-Quantum Digital Signatures

Denis Butin[1]([⊠]), Stefan-Lukas Gazdag[2], and Johannes Buchmann[1]

[1] TU Darmstadt, Darmstadt, Germany
{dbutin,buchmann}@cdc.informatik.tu-darmstadt.de
[2] genua mbH, Kirchheim Bei München, Germany
stefan-lukas_gazdag@genua.eu

Abstract. Digital signatures are ubiquitous in modern security infrastructures. Their lack of diversity in industrial settings makes most contemporary systems susceptible to quantum computer-aided attacks. Alternatives exist, among which a family of well-understood schemes with minimal security requirements: hash-based signatures. In addition to being quantum-safe, hash-based signatures are modular, providing long-term security. They are not yet being used in practice. We discuss the reasons for this gap between theory and practice and outline a strategy to bridge it. We then detail our work to realise the described plan.

Keywords: Authenticity · Post-quantum · Usability · Integration

1 Context and Motivation

Digital signatures are massively used in contemporary security infrastructures. A typical use case is the authentication of software updates, protecting the users of the software from the execution of malicious code. Another common application of digital signatures is server authentication in the Transport Layer Security (TLS) protocol, combined with the Hypertext Transfer Protocol in HTTPS.

Given the sheer amount and diversity of sensitive information transmitted online, robust security of digital signatures is essential. Security protocols such as TLS are typically not tied to any particular type of digital signature. For instance, the TLS protocol merely specifies functional requirements for its cipher suite. However, in practice, common security protocols are only instantiated with a small number of different signature schemes: RSA [43], DSA [19] and its elliptic curve variant ECDSA [31]. Due to the constant progress of cryptanalysis, this lack of diversity alone is already dangerous. Key size itself — assuming only brute-force attacks — is not the most worrying issue, since future computational power can be predicted with reasonable accuracy [33]. Nevertheless, more efficient and elaborate attacks may always emerge. Another more general issue will become increasingly problematic in the future: the classes of security assumptions of these three digital signature schemes.

Indeed, RSA, DSA and ECDSA all rely on the hardness of two mathematical problems: prime number factorisation and discrete logarithm computation.

© Springer International Publishing Switzerland 2015
F. Cleary and M. Felici (Eds.): CSP Forum 2015, CCIS 530, pp. 41–52, 2015.
DOI: 10.1007/978-3-319-25360-2_4

These two problems are susceptible to attacks using quantum computers. In fact, a 1994 algorithm by Shor [45] shows that the two aforementioned problems can be solved in polynomial time with respect to the input size on a quantum computer. Simply increasing key sizes will therefore not be a solution, and this exponential speed-up vis-à-vis classical computers will break RSA, DSA and ECDSA in practice.

While quantum computers capable of yielding such attacks do not yet exist, rapid progress is being made [14]. The energy storage time of quantum switches is increasing vastly [41]. Quantum bit storage time is also growing [44]. In addition, reports mention undisclosed work on quantum computers by governmental intelligence agencies [42]. Even under the optimistic assumption that progress will slow down and that the advent of quantum computers is still far-off, a precautionary approach to risk management demands post-quantum security infrastructures. In particular, post-quantum digital signatures schemes ought to be deployed on a large scale.

Fortunately, several types of post-quantum digital signature schemes already exist. Somewhat surprisingly, some of them have existed for decades but none of them enjoys widespread use. Often, initial performance and storage drawbacks have dampened practical use and interest. This paper focuses on a specific family of post-quantum digital signatures: hash-based signatures (HBS). Reasons for this choice, such as their modularity, are detailed in Sect. 2. Several alternatives exist. All of them face obstacles to widespread deployment. Code-based signatures [13] suffer from excessively large space requirements for keys. More investigations into the operation and security of multivariate-based signatures [15] are needed. Lattice-based signatures [18] such as NTRUSign have been implemented and even patented. A number of strong attacks have been found [37], but since lattice-based signatures are continuously improving, they embody the best current post-quantum alternative to HBS.

Nevertheless, lattice-based signatures do not enjoy the advantages that HBS do. These are detailed in Sect. 2.

1.1   Contributions

The goal of this paper is to identify why post-quantum signatures are not being widely used yet, to outline a remedial strategy and to discuss current project work [21] to realise this plan. To this end, we start by describing HBS and arguments in favour of their use (Sect. 2). We then emphasise the numerous gaps still existing between theory and practice (Sect. 3), notably the shortage of concepts for dealing with stateful key management, the lack of standardisation and the absence of integration in cryptographic software libraries. The main part of the paper outlines a strategy to ready HBS for the real world and discusses our first steps to enact it (Sect. 4). Software integration, both in terms of core implementations in cryptographic libraries such as OpenSSL and in terms of corresponding protocol implementations, is an essential aspect. Standardisation efforts are described with an emphasis on strategic decisions. Parameter selection, use cases and performance improvement opportunities are discussed as well. We conclude with an outlook on future steps (Sect. 5).

2 Hash-Based Signatures

We now recall the main properties of modern HBS. Their elementary building block is the use of a One-Time Signature (OTS) scheme. Many OTS key pairs are combined in a so-called *Merkle Tree* using a hash tree. Several improvements upon the plain Merkle construction have made it much more efficient. Modern HBS variants can be seen as the result of these three building phases, detailed below. We also emphasise important advantages of HBS with respect to other post-quantum signatures: their minimal security requirements and modularity.

2.1 OTS Schemes

OTS schemes are digital signature constructions in themselves, but any OTS signature reveals part of the associated secret key. As a consequence, every OTS secret key can only be used once. Indeed, a second signature using the same key would reveal even more about the key, allowing further signatures to be forged. Two well-known OTS schemes are the Lamport-Diffie scheme [32] and the Winternitz scheme [16]. Their structure is similar, and their security requirement reduces to the collision resistance of the used hash function. In both cases, signing keys are randomly generated and the corresponding verification key is obtained by applying a one-way function (repeatedly, in the Winternitz case) to the signing key. As is usual for signature schemes, in both cases, signatures on a message are actually applied on the hash of the message.

The Winternitz OTS can be seen as a generalization of the Lamport-Diffie OTS. It features the so-called *Winternitz parameter*, which regulates a speed/size trade-off — between signature and key sizes on one hand, and between signature and verification time on the other hand. Lamport-Diffie offers no such flexibility. Modern HBS schemes all use either the Winternitz OTS, or one of its variants. The W-OTS⁺ variant provides a tight security proof despite more modest security requirements on the underlying hash function. A resulting benefit is that W-OTS⁺ is not threatened by a class of generic attacks (*birthday attacks*) that targets stricter security requirements [26]. For this reason, one can afford to securely use much shorter signatures with W-OTS⁺.

2.2 Merkle Trees

Since an OTS key pair can only be used once securely, several OTS key pairs must be combined in a single structure to yield a usable HBS scheme. This is realised in all HBS schemes by combining several OTS key pairs in one or more (binary) Merkle trees. A Merkle tree [35] is a complete tree relating several OTS key pairs to a single public key — the root of the Merkle tree. Merkle trees are also called hash trees because nodes are computed through hashing and concatenation. The leaves of the tree are the hashed OTS verification keys (i.e. OTS public keys). Signatures contain both an OTS signature and a way to authenticate this OTS signature against the public key of the entire tree.

2.3 Subsequent Improvements

Several improvements upon the plain Merkle scheme have taken place over the last decade [10–12,29]. The two most advanced of them are XMSS (the eXtended Merkle Signature Scheme) [10] and XMSS^{MT} (Multi Tree XMSS) [29]. We do not go into technical detail here but explain the main conceptual developments.

A major disadvantage of the initial proposal was the very large signing key size. Successive improvements have curbed this issue. In particular, the use of multiple hash trees (arranged in layers) to combine more OTS key pairs into a single structure enables an amount of OTS key pairs so large as to be plentiful for all practical purposes (e.g. 2^{80} OTS key pairs). OTS signing key storage requirements are dramatically reduced by using a pseudo-random number generator to obtain them in succession. It is then sufficient to store the generation seed value instead of all OTS signing keys. In some variants, signature generation times are reduced by distributing OTS generation and other computations evenly across steps. In schemes such as XMSS [10], it is possible to reduce the requirement on the underlying hash function. Shorter hash length requirements can then be used. Figure 1 depicts an XMSS Merkle tree.

2.4 Forward Security

HBS schemes can provide a valuable property: forward security [4]. The fact that schemes like XMSS or XMSS^{MT} can be forward secure means that all signatures generated before a key compromise remain valid. This attribute supports a form

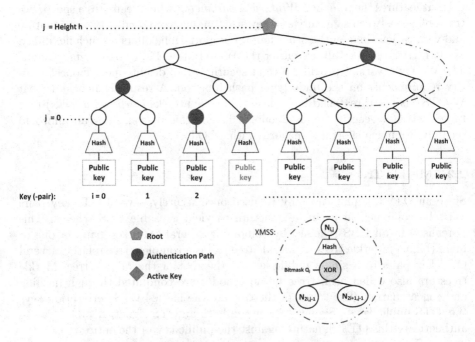

Fig. 1. An XMSS Merkle tree, following Hülsing's [25] description.

of long-term security.[1] Note that forward security is not an intrinsic property of HBS; it requires special constructs such as the use of a pseudo-random number generator. Since these constructs also provide other advantages (such as reduced storage requirements), there is much incentive to use them.

2.5 Further Advantages of Hash-Based Signatures

HBS enjoy a number of other advantages that motivate their deployment. A key aspect is the minimality of their security requirements. Indeed, all types of digital signatures require a secure hash function; yet, in the case of HBS, this requirement is sufficient to ensure overall security. This lack of additional assumptions reduces the security trust requirements.

Furthermore, the OTS scheme that forms the elementary building block of a HBS scheme — be it Lamport-Diffie or Winternitz — is not tied to any specific hash function. The chosen hash function only needs to be secure. This advantage is significant, because it means that HBS schemes are like templates: they may be instantiated with any secure hash function without changing their overall structure. Since hash functions have limited lifespans, this contributes to the longevity of HBS. It is an argument for long-term security: implementations of HBS schemes can be modified to use a more modern hash function without major structural modifications.

The reliance of HBS schemes on a secure hash function works as an early warning system [9]: once attacks on a hash function begin to emerge, a significant amount of time passes until the hash function's security is completely broken. This is especially true when an advanced OTS scheme such as W-OTS$^+$ is used. The kind of attack that threatens W-OTS$^+$ only emerges after attacks on stricter security requirements appear.[2] When first attacks occur, HBS schemes can be updated using a better hash function without major infrastructure modifications. By contrast, for other (non-modular) signature schemes, an attack may entirely compromise the scheme, requiring a switch to a completely different scheme. Such a change is more cumbersome than the mere replacement of a hash function.

3   Obstacles to Widespread Use

It can be seen from the previous section that the theory underlying HBS is well-understood. Moreover, subsequent improvements have solved the performance issues that were an obstacle for more primitive HBS schemes. Even proof-of-concept implementations exist. However, we contend that many steps are still

---

[1] While the full descriptions of XMSS and its multi-tree variant are provably forward secure [10,29], this property relies on constructs irrelevant to interoperability. The proposed standardisation of HBS schemes we discuss later therefore does not intrinsically yield forward security, but permits it if the right components (such as a forward secure pseudo-random number generator) are used in its implementation.

[2] When using W-OTS$^+$, security requirements are reduced from collision resistance to second preimage resistance.

needed if HBS are to become widely used. This section describes the main road-blocks. In the remainder of the paper, we will present a detailed strategy to overcome the outstanding issues.

3.1 Statefulness

Since HBS always depend on OTS schemes, they must keep track of which OTS signing keys have already been used. Using an OTS signing key more than once is insecure. A global key index is therefore used. When a signature is generated, an updated secret key is output too.

As a consequence, HBS schemes are said to be *stateful*. Statefulness is inconvenient in practice for a number of reason. First, it does not fit common software interfaces. Second, performance is impacted by frequent key access. Besides, key storage conditions become critical. Copies or backups containing keys, and old key states in general, must be avoided for security reasons. These concrete consequences need to be taken into account when developing mitigation strategies. Dealing with statefulness is an integral part of the solutions described later (Sect. 4), even though we focus on more high-level issues in this paper. Stateless HBS, based on random index selection and a few-time signature scheme, have recently been introduced [5] to circumvent this issue. We stick to stateful HBS for performance reasons. Another argument in their favour is forward security.

3.2 Lack of Standardisation

All currently popular digital signature schemes have been standardised. RSA, DSA and ECDSA are standardised in the Digital Signature Standard by NIST [36]. Stakeholders prefer to use standardised security techniques. The standardisation process guarantees increased investigation by experts. For instance, the scrutiny resulting from the selection process for the SHA-3 hash function [6] has resulted in over a dozen of cryptanalytic papers on KECCAK [8,17]. Standards usually include security parameter recommendations. This point is especially important for cryptographic schemes that use numerous different parameters. While an abundance of parameters normally allows for greater flexibility and trade-off opportunities, it also considerably increases the complexity of the decision process and makes unforeseeable consequences more likely. Typical parameter sets, especially when coupled with descriptions of typical use cases, offer stakeholders practical, ready-to-go solutions with established guarantees. Additionally, standards are more ergonomic than research publications for means of implementation. The usual tone of standards requires a level of explicitness that is not always found in research literature, but which is indispensable for implementers. Research-oriented descriptions of cryptographic schemes may also use abstract constructions without clarifying which concrete methods may be used to instantiate them. For instance, the initial description of XMSS [10] prescribes the use of a pseudo-random function family. In practice (i.e. for concrete implementations), a secure hash-function provides the functionality of this function family.

3.3   Missing Availability in Commonly Used Software Libraries

Stakeholders should not be expected to adopt new schemes, whatever their advantages, if system integration is too experimental. In the case of HBS, implementations exist [10,27], but they are standalone. While such proof-of-concept implementations are an important, necessary step towards widespread use, it is inopportune for organisations to create their own, specific ad hoc implementations. Avoiding case-by-case implementation of cryptographic primitives is common advice. Instead, well-known and tested cryptographic libraries ought to be used. These libraries include abstractions to facilitate system integration and combination. A well-known example is OpenSSL [1], an open-source library providing not only core implementations of cryptographic primitives, but also their combination in commonly used protocols such as TLS.

4   Bridging the Gap

Standardisation, integration into common cryptographic libraries and the definition of typical use cases and parameters are expected to support the adoption of HBS by increasing clarity, providing interoperability and decreasing costs for organisations.

4.1   Standardisation

An Internet-Draft for the basic Merkle HBS scheme exists [34]. To make further improvements to the scheme widely available, an extension covering the techniques named above is desirable. Therefore, a standard covering the main aspects of newer HBS variants is necessary. We are contributing to an IETF Internet-Draft [28] covering XMSS and its multi-tree variant $XMSS^{MT}$. Some strategic considerations are explained in the current section.

As the underlying OTS scheme, we picked W-OTS$^+$ [26]. As explained earlier, all current efficient OTS schemes are variants of Winternitz's initial proposal. The reason for this choice are the shorter signatures obtained when using W-OTS$^+$, together with improved security guarantees.

The standard proposal will include the pivotal algorithms for XMSS and $XMSS^{MT}$. Regarding XMSS, functions for signing, verification and public key generation are defined. In addition, using the previous one, a function is defined to construct tree leaves from OTS public keys. Another crucial auxiliary algorithm computes the inner nodes. These two functions, in turn, are building blocks of the algorithms for signature generation, checking and public key computation. The use of a pseudo-random number generator for key generation was mentioned in Sect. 2. This aspect is not part of the standard, since its scope is limited to features relevant to interoperability.

XMSS is a building block of $XMSS^{MT}$. As a consequence, the algorithms for $XMSS^{MT}$ signing, verification and public key generation in the standard proposal use the corresponding XMSS algorithms as subroutines. Normally, $XMSS^{MT}$

supports the selection of a different Winternitz parameter on every layer. The Winternitz parameter determines how many message bits are signed simultaneously. In the standard proposal to which we contribute, a single Winternitz parameter is used for the entire XMSS^{MT} scheme. The reason for this choice is the resulting simplification of implementation. The cost in terms of flexibility is modest. Similarly, XMSS^{MT} normally allows a different tree height for each layer, but we proscribe a global tree height used for all layers, for the same reasons. Since the SPHINCS stateless HBS uses XMSS as a constituent, the planned standard will also act as a first step towards the standardisation of such schemes. The standardisation of both categories of HBS schemes is beneficial since different use cases will take advantage of their respective strengths.

4.2   Integration in Cryptographic Libraries

To make modern HBS schemes widely available, our strategy is to integrate them with three important security protocols:

- TLS, to be used with transport layer protocols — e.g. with HTTP for HTTPS;
- SSH, e.g. for remote login;
- S/MIME, for email authentication.

All of these security protocols are supported by common cryptographic software libraries. For TLS and SSH integration, we plan to use OpenSSL and OpenSSH. OpenSSL is widely known and used. While serious vulnerabilities have recently been discovered in OpenSSL [39,40], it is being revisited more closely as a result. In addition, forks such as LibreSSL [38] and BoringSSL [22] have emerged; synergy effects between these projects are expected to further tighten implementation security. Since OpenSSH uses OpenSSL, some of the necessary work benefits both the TLS and the SSH integration.

OpenSSL consists of two sub-libraries: a collection of core implementations of cryptographic constructs, and a library implementing the TLS protocol, relying on the other one. Integrating HBS with OpenSSL is therefore a two-step process. We start by providing a core implementation. Once this is done, further work is required to adapt the protocol-level module so the TLS protocol can actually be instantiated with a cipher suite using HBS for authentication. As far as the core implementation is concerned, existing HBS implementations serve as a starting point but cannot be used as is. OpenSSL defines a number of abstractions, such as the EVP high-level interface to cryptographic functions and other APIs. These abstractions must be extended to cope with the peculiarities of HBS. Notably, changes to key handling are required due to the statefulness of HBS.

When integrating HBS in a TLS cipher suite, a natural question is whether an entire cipher suite can be built. Generally speaking, primitives using symmetric cryptography are not significantly threatened by quantum computers because Shor's algorithm [45] cannot be used against them. Symmetric constructions are somewhat vulnerable to another quantum algorithm, by Grover [23]; but the resulting speed-up is much less threatening. Doubling the key length is sufficient to counteract the threat and to keep the same security level as before. As a consequence, the symmetric primitives used in TLS cipher suites do not need to be replaced for the cipher suite to be post-quantum as long as key length choices take Grover's algorithm into account. However, the key exchange part ought to be replaced. It typically relies on the Diffie–Hellman method, which relies on the discrete logarithm problem and is therefore susceptible to attacks based on Shor's algorithm. Fortunately, post-quantum key exchanges have been put forward. In particular, a key exchange based on the Ring Learning With Errors problem has already been demonstrated in an OpenSSL fork implementation [7]. Combining this implementation with an HBS-based key exchange will yield a post-quantum TLS cipher suite.

The S/MIME standard defines encryption and signing of email messages using the MIME format. S/MIME is also available in OpenSSL, but we plan to integrate HBS with this protocol using a different cryptographic software library: Bouncy Castle [2]. As in OpenSSL, a prerequisite to security protocol integration (S/MIME in this case) is the availability of a HBS as a core implementation. Some preliminary work already exists here, since the GMSS HBS scheme was implemented in Flexiprovider [46], a set of cryptographic modules for the Java Cryptography Architecture. Flexiprovider was later integrated into Bouncy Castle. A more advanced scheme than GMSS is suitable for S/MIME (as well as for the other mentioned protocols). S/MIME uses the Cryptographic Message Syntax (CMS), and Bouncy Castle provides a CMS implementation, which must be adapted to HBS. Fortunately, an Internet-Draft on integration HBS in the CMS already exists [24], and can be used for initial guidance. To further encourage the use of post-quantum S/MIME based on HBS, we intend to wrap the Bouncy Castle HBS S/MIME implementation in a new email client plug-in.

The SSH protocol is used for securing communication and remote login between two hosts. Since OpenSSH is based in part on OpenSSL, the core implementation (independently of the protocol layer) is expected to be straightforward. For SSH integration using OpenSSH, we face cipher suite integration again. The signature part of the cipher suite, which often uses the ECDSA pre-quantum algorithms, will be replaced with a HBS implementation. In addition, once more, a fully post-quantum cipher suite would be sensible. The Diffie-Hellman method or RSA are normally used for SSH key exchange; both are non-quantum-safe. A post-quantum replacement key exchange is therefore needed [20]. Besides, the consequences of situations such as signing key depletion or compromise must be planned for, and public key infrastructures used by the modified protocol adapted in consequence.

4.3   Parameter Selection, Use Cases and Performance

Advanced HBS schemes feature numerous parameters. This is beneficial in terms of flexibility, but makes parameter setting decisions more complex. There is no one parameter set that ought to be recommended in general; rather, different parameter sets are optimal for different use cases. We will define a number of different typical use cases and suggest corresponding parameter sets. Research already exists on semi-automated parameter selection. In a 2013 paper [29], Hülsing describes a method to determine optimal parameters for XMSS^{MT} using exact linear optimisation and IBM'S ILOG CPLEX tool [30], a mathematical programming solver. Results are provided for two use cases. A similar approach must be applied to the XMSS variant. Variations between use cases include requirements in terms of signature generation frequency. Signing speed is much more of a factor in scenarios such as TLS connection management than for e.g. software update authentication, were signature generations and verifications are less frequent. A larger, more fine-grained array of use cases should be investigated.

On a related note, in terms of performance improvements, other opportunities such as the use of instruction set extensions have not yet been fully taken advantage of. Consider for instance current work by de Oliveira on faster XMSS implementation using AVX vector instructions [3].

To obtain a concrete assessment of real-world performance for a specific use case, we are implementing an HBS version of an existing update authentication tool. Since the tool is used to verify the integrity of software patches on client systems, the use case is a low-frequency signing scenario. The authentication tool uses the OpenSSL core cryptographic library; RSA signatures are replaced by XMSS / XMSS^{MT} signatures in the post-quantum version.

5   Conclusions

HBS ought to become widely available in security infrastructures to help counter the threat posed by quantum computers. In this paper, we have argued that while HBS are well-understood by the cryptographic research community, many efforts are still required to foster their use in the real world. In practice, we have insisted on the importance of standardisation and integration in common cryptographic software libraries and security protocol implementations. We have also described current work to support these goals. Standards and reference implementations play an ergonomic role for system integrators and facilitate both technical interfacing and strategic decisions such as parameter selection. They must not be neglected if broad adoption is desired. The intensified debate and technical scrutiny resulting from the engagement with standardisation bodies and library developers serves the goal of greater security shared by all stakeholders.

References

1. OpenSSL: The Open Source toolkit for SSL/TLS. https://www.openssl.org/
2. Legion of the Bouncy Castle (2013). https://www.bouncycastle.org/
3. de Oliveira, A.K.D.S.: An efficient software implementation of XMSS. Presented at LATINCRYPT 2014 (2014)
4. Bellare, M., Miner, S.K.: A forward-secure digital signature scheme. In: Wiener, M. (ed.) CRYPTO 1999. LNCS, vol. 1666, p. 431. Springer, Heidelberg (1999)

5. Bernstein, D.J., et al.: SPHINCS: practical stateless hash-based signatures. In: Oswald, E., Fischlin, M. (eds.) EUROCRYPT 2015. LNCS, vol. 9056, pp. 368–397. Springer, Heidelberg (2015)
6. Bertoni, G., Daemen, J., Peeters, M., Assche, G.V.: The KECCAK reference (2011). http://keccak.noekeon.org/
7. Bos, J.W., Costello, C., Naehrig, M., Stebila, D.: Post-quantum key exchange for the TLS protocol from the ring learning with errors problem. IEEE Symposium on Security and Privacy, pp. 553-570 (2015)
8. Boura, C., Canteaut, A.: Zero-sum distinguishers for iterated permutations and application to Keccak-f and Hamsi-256. In: Biryukov, A., Gong, G., Stinson, D.R. (eds.) SAC 2010. LNCS, vol. 6544, pp. 1–17. Springer, Heidelberg (2011)
9. Braun, J., Hülsing, A., Wiesmaier, A., Vigil, M.A.G., Buchmann, J.: How to avoid the breakdown of public key infrastructures. In: De Capitani di Vimercati, S., Mitchell, C. (eds.) EuroPKI 2012. LNCS, vol. 7868, pp. 53–68. Springer, Heidelberg (2013)
10. Buchmann, J., Dahmen, E., Hülsing, A.: XMSS - a practical forward secure signature scheme based on minimal security assumptions. In: Yang, B.-Y. (ed.) PQCrypto 2011. LNCS, vol. 7071, pp. 117–129. Springer, Heidelberg (2011)
11. Buchmann, J., Dahmen, E., Klintsevich, E., Okeya, K., Vuillaume, C.: Merkle signatures with virtually unlimited signature capacity. In: Katz, J., Yung, M. (eds.) ACNS 2007. LNCS, vol. 4521, pp. 31–45. Springer, Heidelberg (2007)
12. Buchmann, J., García, L.C.C., Dahmen, E., Döring, M., Klintsevich, E.: CMSS – an improved Merkle signature scheme. In: Barua, R., Lange, T. (eds.) INDOCRYPT 2006. LNCS, vol. 4329, pp. 349–363. Springer, Heidelberg (2006)
13. Courtois, N.T., Finiasz, M., Sendrier, N.: How to achieve a McEliece-based digital signature scheme. In: Boyd, C. (ed.) ASIACRYPT 2001. LNCS, vol. 2248, p. 157. Springer, Heidelberg (2001)
14. DeAngelis, S.F.: Closing In On Quantum Computing. Wired (2014)
15. Ding, J., Schmidt, D.: Rainbow, a new multivariable polynomial signature scheme. In: Ioannidis, J., Keromytis, A.D., Yung, M. (eds.) ACNS 2005. LNCS, vol. 3531, pp. 164–175. Springer, Heidelberg (2005)
16. Dods, C., Smart, N.P., Stam, M.: Hash based digital signature schemes. In: Smart, N.P. (ed.) Cryptography and Coding 2005. LNCS, vol. 3796, pp. 96–115. Springer, Heidelberg (2005)
17. Duc, A., Guo, J., Peyrin, T., Wei, L.: Unaligned rebound attack: application to Keccak. In: Canteaut, A. (ed.) FSE 2012. LNCS, vol. 7549, pp. 402–421. Springer, Heidelberg (2012)
18. Ducas, L., Durmus, A., Lepoint, T., Lyubashevsky, V.: Lattice signatures and bimodal gaussians. In: Canetti, R., Garay, J.A. (eds.) CRYPTO 2013, Part I. LNCS, vol. 8042, pp. 40–56. Springer, Heidelberg (2013)
19. El Gamal, T.: A public key cryptosystem and a signature scheme based on discrete logarithms. In: Blakely, G.R., Chaum, D. (eds.) CRYPTO 1984. LNCS, vol. 196, pp. 10–18. Springer, Heidelberg (1985)
20. ETSI: White paper: Quantum Safe Cryptography and Security; An introduction, benefits, enablers and challenges. http://docbox.etsi.org/Workshop/2014/201410_CRYPTO/Quantum_Safe_Whitepaper_1_0_0.pdf (2014)
21. Gazdag, S., Butin, D.: Practical Hash-based Signatures (Quantencomputer-resistente Signaturverfahren für die Praxis) (2014). http://square-up.org/
22. Google: BoringSSL (2014). https://boringssl.googlesource.com/boringssl/
23. Grover, L.K.: A fast quantum mechanical algorithm for database search. In: Symposium on Theory of Computing (STOC), pp. 212–219. ACM (1996)

24. Housley, R.: Use of the hash-based Merkle tree signature (MTS) algorithm in the cryptographic message syntax (CMS). IETF (2015) (Internet-Draft)
25. Hülsing, A.: Practical Forward Secure Signatures using Minimal Security Assumptions. Ph.D. thesis, Technische Universität Darmstadt (2013)
26. Hülsing, A.: W-OTS+ – shorter signatures for hash-based signature schemes. In: Youssef, A., Nitaj, A., Hassanien, A.E. (eds.) AFRICACRYPT 2013. LNCS, vol. 7918, pp. 173–188. Springer, Heidelberg (2013)
27. Hülsing, A., Busold, C., Buchmann, J.: Forward secure signatures on smart cards. In: Knudsen, L.R., Wu, H. (eds.) SAC 2012. LNCS, vol. 7707, pp. 66–80. Springer, Heidelberg (2013)
28. Hülsing, A., Butin, D., Gazdag, S.L., Mohaisen, A.: XMSS: Extended Hash-Based Signatures. IETF (2015) (Internet-Draft)
29. Hülsing, A., Rausch, L., Buchmann, J.: Optimal parameters for $XMSS^{MT}$. In: Cuzzocrea, A., Kittl, C., Simos, D.E., Weippl, E., Xu, L. (eds.) CD-ARES Workshops 2013. LNCS, vol. 8128, pp. 194–208. Springer, Heidelberg (2013)
30. IBM: IBM ILOG CPLEX Optimizer. http://www-01.ibm.com/software/commerce/optimization/cplex-optimizer/index.html
31. Johnson, D., Menezes, A., Vanstone, S.: The elliptic curve digital signature algorithm (ECDSA). Int. J. Inf. Secur. 1(1), 36–63 (2001)
32. Lamport, L.: Constructing Digital Signatures from a One Way Function. Technical report, SRI International Computer Science Laboratory (1979)
33. Lenstra, A.K., Verheul, E.R.: Selecting cryptographic key sizes. J. Crypt. 14(4), 255–293 (2001)
34. McGrew, D., Curcio, M.: Hash-Based Signatures. IETF (2014) (Internet-Draft)
35. Merkle, R.C.: A certified digital signature. In: Brassard, G. (ed.) CRYPTO 1989. LNCS, vol. 435, pp. 218–238. Springer, Heidelberg (1990)
36. National Institute of Standards and Technology: FIPS PUB 186–4: Digital Signature Standard (DSS). National Institute for Standards and Technology (2013). http://nvlpubs.nist.gov/nistpubs/FIPS/NIST.FIPS.186-4.pdf
37. Nguyen, P.Q., Regev, O.: Learning a parallelepiped: cryptanalysis of GGH and NTRU signatures. J. Crypt. 22(2), 139–160 (2009)
38. OpenBSD: LibreSSL (2014). http://www.libressl.org/
39. OpenSSL Security Advisory: SSL/TLS MITM vulnerability (CVE-2014-0224) (2014). https://www.openssl.org/news/secadv_20140605.txt
40. OpenSSL Security Advisory: TLS heartbeat read overrun (CVE-2014-0160) (2014). https://www.openssl.org/news/secadv/20140407.txt
41. Pop, I.M., Geerlings, K., Catelani, G., Schoelkopf, R.J., Glazman, L.I., Devoret, M.H.: Coherent suppression of electromagnetic dissipation due to superconducting quasiparticles. Nat. 508(7496), 369–372 (2014)
42. Rich, S., Gellman, B.: NSA seeks to build quantum computer that could crack most types of encryption. The Washington Post (2014)
43. Rivest, R., Shamir, A., Adleman, L.: A method for obtaining digital signatures and public-key cryptosystems. Commun. ACM 21, 120–126 (1978)
44. Saeedi, K., et al.: Room-temperature quantum bit storage exceeding 39 minutes using ionized donors in silicon-28. Sci. 342(6160), 830–833 (2013)
45. Shor, P.W.: Polynomial-time algorithms for prime factorization and discrete logarithms on a quantum computer. SIAM J. Comput. 26(5), 1484–1509 (1997)
46. TU Darmstadt: FlexiProvider, an open source Java Cryptographic Service Provider (2006). http://www.flexiprovider.de/javadoc/flexiprovider/docs/de/flexiprovider/pqc/hbc/gmss/package-summary.html

Security and Privacy in Vehicular Communications with INTER-TRUST

Juan M. Marín Pérez[1]([✉]), Antonio Moragón Juan[1], Jaime Arrazola Pérez[2],
Javier Monge Rabadán[2], and Antonio F. Skarmeta Gómez[1]

[1] Department of Information and Communications Engineering,
University of Murcia, Murcia, Spain
{juanmanuel,amoragon,skarmeta}@um.es
[2] Department of Infrastructures, Indra Sistemas S.A., Alcobendas, Spain
{jarrazola,jmonger}@indra.es

Abstract. Security systems in Intelligent Transport Systems (ITS) are
woefully underprepared for the security threats in the modern landscape.
However, the real potential for loss of life in the event of a successful
attack makes these systems the more important to protect against such
intrusions. In this paper, a new security framework that is the result of
the INTER-TRUST European project will be presented and proposed as
a solution that could solve most of ITS's current security problems. The
solution provides dynamic and adaptable security with a set of monitoring tools that also enable the adaptation of security to different contexts
or situations that makes away with the need to recode the original applications. An overview on ITS security and how specific security features
can be provided to ITS applications by deploying the INTER-TRUST
framework is analyzed. A proof of concept implementation has been also
developed during this research with some experimental results.

Keywords: Security · Privacy · ITS · Policy-based · AOP · INTER-
TRUST

1   Introduction

No longer bound by the limits of human control, vehicles and the infrastructures
they rely on are becoming increasingly smart enough to take over for the driver
and in doing so enhance our mobility, sustainability and safety. This has brought
forth the advent of Intelligent Transport Systems, currently culminating in some
of the most ambitious projects of the last decades, such as driverless cars.

However, the fact that most, if not all, major ITS deployments rely on IP-
based technologies, and more often than not on communication through wireless
interfaces, makes ITS technologies a near-certain target of the types of attacks
that are becoming an everyday occurrence in other fields. Reading up on the
literature surrounding ITS systems, it becomes quickly apparent that there has
been surprisingly little effort made until recently in scientific circles to secure

© Springer International Publishing Switzerland 2015
F. Cleary and M. Felici (Eds.): CSP Forum 2015, CCIS 530, pp. 53–64, 2015.
DOI: 10.1007/978-3-319-25360-2_5

such systems, despite the potential for catastrophic consequences if such security measures are not developed and implemented in a conscientious manner.

In this article, a new security framework that is the result of the INTER-TRUST European project [9] will be presented and proposed as a solution that could solve most of ITS's current security problems despite the complexity and limits inherent to ITS systems. The proposed solution enables policy-based management of ITS security, resulting in a dynamic and adaptable security solution. The solution endows current ITS applications with security features without need to recode the original applications. The architecture excels at working with dynamic code and facilitates integration through the use of a negotiation mechanism for interoperability of systems with heterogeneous security requirements. It also provides offline and online testing capabilities that allows early detection of vulnerabilities. Finally, a set of monitoring elements also enable the adaptation of security to different contexts or situations according to the specified policies.

This paper is organized as follows. Section 2 presents some related works. Section 3 provides an overview of ITS security. Section 4 explains how security is provided by deploying the INTER-TRUST framework. Section 5 gives details about the proof of concept implementation with some experimental results. Finally, Sect. 6 provides some conclusions and states of direction.

2   Related Work

ITS and cooperative mobility systems involve at their core, communications networks that handle the exchange of information among vehicles and control centers. As such, there is a general consensus [6,16] in the industry that ensuring both security and privacy of ITS communications is currently recognized as a key requirement for a successful deployment of such systems in Europe [5].

Therefore, it is no surprise that the number of ITS related projects have dealt with such issues recently or have ongoing activities in this field is growing and is beginning to form a considerable body of work. Projects like NoW (Network on Wheels), SEVECOM (SEcure VEhicular COMmunications), EVITA (E-safety Vehicle Intrusion Protected Applications), PRECIOSA (Privacy Enabled Capability in Co-operative Systems and Safety Applications), OVERSEE (Open Vehicular Secure Platform) and PRESERVE (Preparing Secure Vehicle-to-X Communication Systems) are contributing to fixing this key barrier to widespread adoption of next-generation ITS systems. These projects focused on the many and varied facets of security and privacy in ITS systems such as: preventing privacy violations and denial of service attacks against the system, while providing V2V authentication broadcast with embedded cryptographic mechanisms and, in order to preserve the driver privacy, the use of changing and revocable pseudonyms. At a higher level, there is work being done by several global engineering organizations and standards bodies. Amongst these, IEEE P1609.2 standard [8] as part of the DSRC (Dedicated Short Range Communications) family of standards for vehicular communications, proposes the use of asymmetric cryptography to sign safety messages with frequently changing keys so that anonymity is preserved. In the field of institution-based standards, both ISO (CALM family of standards [11]) and ETSI (ITS family of standards, in particular ETSI TS 103 097 [4]) form the bulk of the efforts made to support the deployment of efficient security measures in ITS in Europe and the US.

While security implications have came largely as an after-thought, there is a growing trend to address security in the context of the future of ITS. As a result, very recent work on vehicular cloud networks [12], implications for national security and treating ITS as an infrastructure worth protecting [15] and even in crowd-sourced ITS systems [7] is showing that the ITS security industry is increasing looking forward to prevent instead of backwards to cure the problem. These developments present the real forefront of ITS security and it is encouraging to see such visionary work being done within the field.

3   The Complexity of Securing ITS

The European ITS community has specified a common communication architecture for Cooperative Intelligent Transport Systems (C-ITS) under the action of research projects funded by European programs FP6/FP7, the C2CC and international standardization bodies. The architecture [1,11] has been specially conceived to support a variety of ITS application types and scenarios. It relies on the concept of ITS Station (ITS-S), which represents an interconnected entity that can implement different functionalities on the ITS network. According to the ISO/ETSI station reference architecture, three types of ITS stations could exist. These determine the three principal entities of an ITS environment:

- **Intelligent Vehicle (Vehicle ITS-S).** A vehicle able to communicate with the outside world. An On-Board Unit (OBU) module is in charge of providing network connectivity to in-vehicle hosts (e.g. user interface). Through the OBU, the vehicle accesses ITS services offered by the road operator.
- **Road Operator (Central ITS-S).** Represents the central nervous system of modern road infrastructures. It centralizes data from all the nearby available sensors, aggregates and processes the information, and then act through a range of actuators such as Variable Message Signs.
- **Roadside Unit (Roadside ITS-S).** These are communication hot-spots placed on the road at key points meant to provide secondary, short-range, over-the-air communication capacities between road operators and vehicles.

From the description of the entities above, it is seen that the ITS field is a completely distributed system where vehicular networks interact with fixed points in the infrastructure, road operators and other vehicles in a seamless way which presents clear security issues. In order for some ITS services to work it is necessary to both relay communications securely, and have a guarantee that the data from vehicles is trustworthy. For example, if a vehicle with an attacker is traveling down a busy highway, it would be trivially easy to steal troves of private data from other users if these are not properly secured, by just putting the attacking vehicle in closer proximity to its victim than another vehicle. Also, an attacker could attempt to flood a network for a Denial-of-Service attack or worse, to simulate road conditions that are far from what is in reality so that mobility algorithms re-direct road users away from the optimal route. On another hand, depending on the specific ITS service, one entity can have complete priority over another and vice-versa. Most notably this difference is seen when a safety service, which puts a premium in Vehicle-to-vehicle communications, is used alongside an incident detection and notification system.

An adequate security level in vehicular communications is essential to protect against tampering or impersonation security attacks, which may have disastrous effects in vehicular environments if done on a large scale. Several security objectives should be considered: **confidentiality**, **integrity**, **authenticity**, **access control**, **timeliness** and **privacy**. It is worth mentioning that this summarizes a set of security objectives initially identified by ETSI in [3] that has been extended with other well-known security objectives in information systems [13].

Taking into account the aforementioned ITS entities, the following elements are identified as key assets to be protected:

- **Exchanged Messages.** The system must not allow an intruder or a dishonest driver to attack the integrity of the services or the users by either inserting fake messages or modifying the ITS messages.
- **Identity of the Vehicle.** It is necessary to protect the identity of the vehicle as well as preventing the capture of travel patterns and habits from the drivers, even if their identity is unknown.
- **Sensitive Data.** Sensitive or personal data belonging to the driver should be protected for privacy reasons. This includes any data of the vehicle that could deal with the acquisition of information about the driver.
- **Access to the Service.** Services should be subject to access policies that limit the use of the information provided only to those vehicles and drivers that have the right to access the service.

As an example, let us consider a user Bob, which is driving his car and makes use of a service that recommends optimal speed for a given road. Bob's vehicle is sending Collaborative Awareness Messages (CAM) periodically. These messages include fields like identity of the vehicle, position, speed, acceleration, etc. In turn, the road operator is also sending back messages with the recommended speed. In this scenario, messages should be signed to be protected against undesired modification by any third party, as well as certifying the authenticity of the message being sent by the legitimate sender (i.e. Bob's vehicle or the road operator). Moreover, some fields of messages sent by Bob's vehicle should be also preserved to protect Bob's privacy. For instance, the identity of the vehicle should be changed by a pseudonym in order to avoid traceability and some fields like speed or position can be obfuscated for privacy reasons.

4   Enabling ITS Security with INTER-TRUST

The Interoperable Trust Assurance Infrastructure (INTER-TRUST) project [9] is an European project whose main aim is to develop a framework to support trustworthy applications in heterogeneous networks and devices based on the

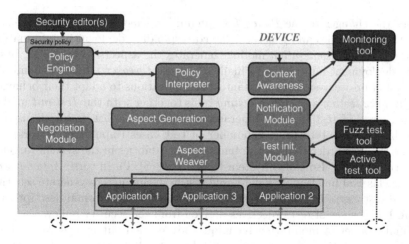

Fig. 1. INTER-TRUST framework architecture overview

enforcement of interoperable and changing security policies. The framework addresses all the steps of modeling and deployment of security requirements, namely: security policy specification; deployment of security modules; component configuration; and, redeployment in case of changes in the environment.

Figure 1 shows an overview of the INTER-TRUST framework. It is composed by several modules that can be grouped into four main blocks of functionality: *Security policy specification*, *Dynamic deployment of security policies*, *Testing techniques for vulnerabilities detection* and *Monitoring techniques*. A description of the framework follows, providing an overview of the functionality carried out by each module and the overall framework depicted in the figure.

Security policy specification is handled by the *Security policy editor*, *Negotiation* and *Security policy engine* modules. Policy definition is done with the *Security policy editor*. The policy lists the security requirements for applications, including conditions that state what happens in different situations, e.g. in case of a security flaw detection. The *Negotiation* module performs two kinds of negotiation: interoperability and trust negotiation. The former can be viewed as a set of negotiated contracts between different entities that are applied to control and regulate their interoperation. The latter is an approach for gradually establishing trust between interacting parties, based on a gradual and bilateral disclosure of information used to prove their trustworthiness. The *Policy engine* acts as a Policy Decision Point (PDP) and manages the security policies.

Dynamic deployment of security policies is performed by the *Policy interpreter*, *Aspects generation*, and *Aspects weaver* modules. This is done by means of Aspect Oriented Programming paradigm [14], which enables injection of code into existing applications without need to change the original code. In brief, an *aspect* is an abstraction of a functionality that may be linked to many parts of a program. Aspects are integrated into the original application in specific locations in a process known as *weaving*. The reader is referred to [14] for more information. In INTER-TRUST, when a policy should be deployed, the *Policy Engine* notifies the changes to the *Policy Interpreter*. This module analyzes and interprets the policy rules and generates the corresponding deployment information. Then, the *Aspects generation* module generates the aspects to be woven, based on the deployment information. Finally, the *Aspect weaver* module dynamically weaves and un-weaves the aspects into the applications to adapt their behavior.

The *Fuzz testing* and *Active testing* tools together with the *Test init* module are in charge of testing and vulnerabilities detection. *Fuzz testing* is used to algorithmically generate a vast number of test cases (input test vectors) and execute them in order to detect potential vulnerabilities in the system target of evaluation (ToE), also called System Under Test (SUT). In turn, *Active testing* extends classical functional model-based testing techniques to generate security-oriented test cases. It generates abstract test cases from a formal description of the SUT and a set of test objectives derived from the security policy.

Finally, a set of monitoring techniques are carried out by the *Notification*, *Monitoring* and *Context awareness* modules. The *Notification* module delivers information about the internal events of the system to the *Monitoring* tool. Notifications target application events that are relevant for security analysis. The *Monitoring* tool correlates events in order to detect security vulnerabilities and non-compliance of security requirements. It generates alarms that provoke the reaction of the system by triggering a new deployment according to the new situation. The *Context awareness* module captures the application environment changes to notify the *Policy engine* and the *Monitoring* tool. This allows to dynamically adapt the deployed security according to the context, which is one of the main objectives of the INTER-TRUST project.

4.1 Deployment in Vehicular Scenario

As exposed in Sect. 3, three principal entities come into play in an ITS environment: Intelligent Vehicle, Road Operator and Roadside Unit (RSU). For the purpose of INTER-TRUST deployment, two main types of administrative domains are distinguished in ITS environments: vehicles and infrastructure, formed by the road operator and roadside units. Both domains interact and require the deployment of two particular instances of the framework. On one hand, each road operator manages the security of its applications at both the Central ITS-S and RSUs. On the other hand, each vehicle is an autonomous entity which requires its own security management, and thereby its particular framework instance.

Figure 2 shows the deployment of the INTER-TRUST framework within the ITS architecture in order to allow the development of secure ITS services. As can be seen, the ITS applications of each vehicle and road operator are managed by a vehicle's own instance of the INTER-TRUST framework. This allows each one to define and control its own set of security policies for its applications. That is, Bob is able to manage the policies of his vehicle, according to his preferences, while the road operator defines the policies for the services it offers. The monitoring and context awareness part of the framework is able to adapt

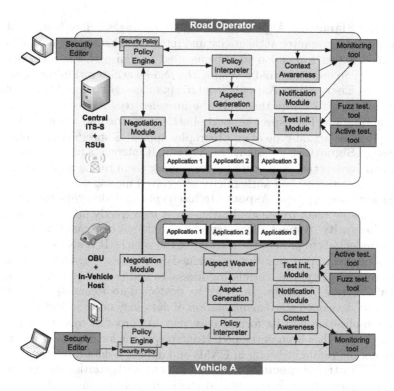

Fig. 2. Deployment of INTER-TRUST framework for ITS

the behavior under different circumstances according to the policies. ITS applications interact with their counterpart in a different entity, exchanging information to provide the service. The interaction among them is also overseen by INTER-TRUST, providing trust management and negotiation capabilities. Although not depicted in the figure for clarity reasons, interaction with other vehicles is done in the same way that for the road operator. It should be also noticed that in this deployment, RSUs have been considered part of the road operator domain. Hence, applications within RSUs are managed by the road operator instance of the framework. This way, an homogeneous policy management can be applied. In case RSUs belong to a different domain, an alternative deployment would deploy a dedicated instance of the framework into each RSU the same way it is deployed within each vehicle.

4.2 Security Features in Vehicular Scenario

As explained in Sect. 4, the INTER-TRUST framework provides security to existing applications by means of aspect weaving using the AOP paradigm. The following aspects have been developed to endow the framework with the proper code module that is needed to provide the required security to ITS applications.

– **Message Signature Aspect.** It intercepts messages before being sent and signs them to guarantee authenticity and integrity. This aspect also takes into account whether a pseudonym is being used to sign with the corresponding private key in order to avoid revealing the real identifier within the signature.
– **Message Encryption Aspect.** It intercepts messages before being sent and encrypts them to assure that only the intended receivers are able to access the information. The aspect supports both symmetric and asymmetric cryptography. The actual type of cryptography applied is specified via policies.
– **Message Signature Verification Aspect.** It intercepts messages on reception and verifies their signature before passing them to the application. This assures the integrity and authenticity of received messages.
– **Message Decryption Aspect.** It intercepts and decrypts the messages before passing them to the application for it to correctly parse the content.
– **Pseudonymity Aspect.** This aspect is in charge of requesting pseudonymous credentials to protect the identity of the vehicle. It is also able to change the pseudonym upon an event determined by policies (e.g. OBU startup) to avoid a third party from correlating messages and trace driver behavior.
– **Data Privacy Aspects.** In order to protect data items, specific aspects should be developed since manipulation of data may occur at different points of the application and its format may vary. As proof of concept, a location privacy aspect has been developed. It intercepts the location provided by the GPS module before inclusion in CAMs and applies a data distortion method.
– **Access Control Aspects.** Authentication and authorization aspects process service requests to authenticate and check the permissions of the requestor. The authorization aspect queries the *Policy Engine* for this to take a decision based on the authorization policies.

These aspects cover the set of security objectives for the ITS assets identified in Sect. 3. The first four cover the security objectives to protect exchanged messages providing confidentiality, integrity and authenticity. With these aspects, messages sent by Bob are protected and the road operator is able to check that they are not modified and have been legitimately sent by Bob. Similarly, Bob can also check messages sent by the road operator. These aspects can be woven to any point in the application where a message is sent. They are designed to intercept a byte array parameter containing the original message and change it with the protected (i.e. encrypted or signed) message. Separated aspects are provided for signing and encrypting. However, they can be combined by weaving them into the same point of the application, which results in the message to be both signed and encrypted.

Regarding privacy, the pseudonymity aspect requests pseudonyms according to the policies defined by Bob for his vehicle. An example of privacy policy would state *"use a pseudonym for vehicle Id"*. Additionally, a policy stating *"change pseudonym on OBU start"* could be also defined to avoid detection of patterns when the same pseudonym is used. These policies would make the framework to deploy the pseudonymity aspect into the OBU. This would request a new pseudonym and use it as identity in message fields. This includes requesting a pseudonymous certificate to be used for signing and encrypting messages.

The INTER-TRUST framework provides a set of tools called *Privacy Preserving Tools* (PPT). It includes a certification authority to generate pseudonymous credentials based on PKI certificates. This is used by the pseudonymity aspect to obtain new credentials. This approach is based on the recommendations from ETSI TS 102 731 [2]. It specifies an *Enrollment Authority* service that vehicles contact to obtain pseudonymous credentials. In our deployment, the certification authority provided by the PPT plays the role of this authority.

A set of transformations for data distortion also are provided by these tools. This enable the definition of policies such as *"obfuscate GPS position by 20 min (in GPS coordinates)"* that would obfuscate the data included in the position field of the messages. Current implementation includes: approximation to N decimal digits, resolution modification, Gaussian and Laplacian Noise Addition, among others. Data privacy aspects use these methods to transform and protect sensible data. Policy rules can determine what method is actually used. The INTER-TRUST API provided to aspect developers enables the retrieval of configuration data derived from policies to customize the behavior of aspects.

It should be noted that privacy involves several aspects working together. Not only the pseudonymity and data privacy aspects are concerned about privacy, but also signature and encryption when securing messages. These aspects should be aware of the current identity, which can be a pseudonym, in order to use the corresponding cryptographic keys. Otherwise, signature verification or decryption would fail or, even worse, reveal the actual identity of the sender.

5   Implementation

A proof of concept implementation has been developed to evaluate the feasibility of the proposal in a realistic service. The mobility-enhancing service commonly known as Contextual Speed Advisory (CSA) has been chosen. It aims at providing drivers with dynamic information about the recommended speed limit on the road in order to maintain maximum mobility. This would reduce stop-and-go situations, thus speeding up the traffic flow and reducing fuel consumption.

The testbed scenario involves the three kinds of ITS stations: vehicle, RSU and Central ITS-S. These are running a set of Java-based OSGi framework applications. Concretely, they run under Java SE 1.7 and *Equinox*, the Eclipse Foundation OSGi implementation, in its version 3.9.1. The original ITS applications used for this research do not provide any security capability. The INTER-TRUST framework has been deployed as described in Sect. 4.1 and aspects developed as in Sect. 4.2. Aspects are woven and configured by the framework according to a security policy defined for the CSA service. AspectJ 1.7.3 version from the Eclipse Foundation has been used for aspect development.

Several tests have been done in the scope of INTER-TRUST for ITS. Negotiation of security policy has been done to achieve interoperability. Active testing with injection of malicious messages has been performed to detect vulnerabilities at deployment time, both before and after policy activation. Monitoring techniques have been tested based on an emergency situation that makes the system to react to an increased security level. Details about these tests are out of the scope of this paper and can be found as part of INTER-TRUST material [10].

In order to obtain performance of adding security features with INTER-TRUST, tests have been done to measure average times needed to deploy different security policies. The testbed run the CSA software and the INTER-TRUST framework over an Intel Core i5 1.6GHz processor with 8 GBs RAM running Arch Linux distribution. For each test, a serie of 50 executions (activations and deactivations) of security policies have been measured.

A set of policy rules has been defined to activate and deactivate security features in the CSA application of the OBU. Concretely, the following rules are considered: message encryption (encrypt), message signature (sign), privacy by hiding a value (hide) and privacy by data distortion (obfuscate). They have been selected because they can be measured without need to wait for a message from the central ITS-S. Combinations of these rules have been considered, resulting in a set of 10 policies with one, two or three security features applied at a time.

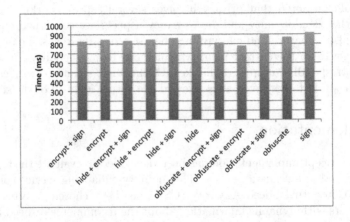

Fig. 3. Security policy deployment times

Figure 3 depicts deployment times for the different policies. Times show the execution of modules involved in the dynamic deployment of policies. That is, the *Policy interpreter*, *Aspects generation*, and *Aspects weaver*. As can be observed, times are homogeneous with small variations around 100 ms. Results do not arise dependence between times and the number of deployed policy rules. It should be noticed that these times do not measure the execution of the security feature, e.g. 'encrypt + sign' does not mean time for encryption and signature, but just time to process the policy rules and activate the associated aspects. The appreciated time variations are probably due to delays in the communication of modules since the framework uses a message broker to this end. Thus, the difference on processing times between one, two or three policy rules are insignificant against communication times and are not appreciated. Further research will be done trying to measure times of individual modules avoiding network delays.

It is worth mentioning that policies are deployed independently by each instance of the framework. This means that deployment time is not affected by the number of vehicles since each vehicle deploys its own policy. Analogously, the road operator also deploys its own policy. This may affect one or more vehicles, but this does not necessarily impacts deployment times. For instance, a policy for message signature is deployed only once, although it signs messages sent to any number of vehicles. It is the performance of some security functionalities what might be affected by the number of vehicles. However, this depends on the aspect implementation and it is out of the scope of the deployment framework.

As average value for a policy deployment, we concretely got 854 ms, which is an acceptable value for such a complex process like deploying a set of security features to an application. Note that this process does not occur every time, but just when a new policy should be applied. Once deployed, the execution of the application suffers no delay in executing the security features.

6 Conclusion

The proposed solution endows ITS applications with security, based on the INTER-TRUST framework. Security is provided following a dynamic approach with reconfiguration capabilities that enables the adaptation of security according to changes in the context reported by a monitoring subsystem. It yields high value to ITS scenarios, which present a highly dynamic and changing environment. Management of security through policies with support for policy conflict analysis aids enhancing the security of the system. Security is injected into existing applications following an AOP paradigm, which avoids the need to change the entire application. The framework also provides a set of testing tools that allow to test the security. This reduces the risk of introducing new vulnerabilities or failures when providing security to existing applications. A proof of concept implementation has been developed and performance results have been obtained, resulting in reasonable times for deployment of security policies.

INTER-TRUST provides a security solution that can be also applied to other areas and fields beyond ITS. Within the project, it has been applied to an electronic voting platform, where security of elections is managed. Other fields of interest include the Internet of Things, where connected devices would benefit from policy negotiation to interoperate; or biomedical systems, where alignment and modification of the security policies is often required by changes in legislative requirements or by the need of interoperation among different health care centres.

The solution still has room for growth in the short term, such as in the creation of generic security aspects that could be readily deployed in cross-domain solutions, the automatic or programatic inclusion of testing and monitoring tools in newly applied security aspects. In the long term, there is great potential for growth in the semantic interpretation of security policies to greatly facilitate the implementation of security capabilities by non-experts in a system.

Acknowledgments. This work has been partially funded by the project *Interoperable Trust Assurance Infrastructure* (INTER-TRUST - ICT FP7 - G.A. 317731). European Commission 7th Framework Programme (FP7-ICT-2011-8).

References

1. ETSI EN 302 665: Intelligent Transport Systems (ITS); Communications Architecture. European standard (telecommunications series), European Telecommunications Standards Institute (2010)
2. ETSI TS 102 731: Intelligent Transport Systems (ITS); Security; Security Services and Architecture. Technical specification, European Telecommunications Standards Institute (2010)
3. ETSI TS 102 940: Intelligent Transport Systems (ITS); Security; ITS communications security architecture and security management. Technical specification, European Telecommunications Standards Institute (2012)
4. ETSI TS 103 097: Intelligent Transport Systems (ITS); Security; Security header and certificate formats. Technical specification, European Telecommunications Standards Institute (2013)
5. European Commission: The European Communications Architecture for Co-operative Systems - Summary Document. Technical report, European Commission, Information Society & Media DG (2009)
6. Foss, T.: Safe and secure intelligent transport systems (ITS). In: Transport Research Arena (TRA) 2014 Proceedings. Paris, France (2014)
7. Friginal, J., Gambs, S., Guiochet, J., Killijian, M.O.: Towards privacy-driven design of a dynamic carpooling system. Pervasive Mob. Comput. **14**, 71–82 (2014)
8. IEEE 1609.2-2013: IEEE Standard for Wireless Access in Vehicular Environments Security Services for Applications and Management Messages. Ieee standard, Institute of Electrical and Electronics Engineers (2013)
9. INTER-TRUST project: Interoperable Trust Assurance Infrastructure. http://inter-trust.eu
10. INTER-TRUST project: D5.4 - final evaluation report. Technical report, INTER-TRUST (2015)
11. ISO 21217:2014: Intelligent transport systems - Communications access for land mobiles (CALM) - Architecture. Standard, International Organization for Standardization (2014)
12. Rajbhoj, S.K., Chandre, P.R.: Implementation of enhanced security on vehicular cloud computing. Int. J. Comput. Sci. Inf. Technol. (IJCSIT) **5**(2), 1315–1318 (2014)
13. Menezes, A.J., van Oorschot, P.C., Vanstone, S.A.: Handbook of Applied Cryptography, 5th edn. CRC Press, Boca Raton (2001)
14. Walls, C., Breidenbach, R.: Spring in Action. Manning Publications Co., Greenwich (2007)
15. Yeganegi, K., Panah, M.A., Bagheri, Z.: The position of intelligent transportation system in national security. WALIA J. **30**(S2), 170–175 (2014)
16. Zhao, M., Walker, J., Wang, C.C.: Challenges and opportunities for securing intelligent transportation system. IEEE J. Emerg. Sel. Top. Circuit Syst. **3**(1), 96–105 (2013)

Towards the Dynamic Provision of Virtualized Security Services

Cataldo Basile, Christian Pitscheider, Fulvio Risso,
Fulvio Valenza$^{(\boxtimes)}$, and Marco Vallini

Dipartimento Automatica e Informatica, Politecnico di Torino, Turin, Italy
{cataldo.basile,christian.pitscheider,fulvio.risso,
fulvio.valenza,marco.vallini}@polito.it

Abstract. Network operators face several limitations in terms of infrastructure management and costs when trying to offer security services to a large number of customers with current technologies. Network Functions Virtualization and Software-Defined Networks paradigms try to overcome these limitations by allowing more flexibility, configurability and agility. Unfortunately, the problem of deciding which security services to use, where to place and how to configure them is a multi-dimensional problem that has no easy solution. This paper provides a model that can be used to determine the best allocation for the security applications needed to satisfy the user requirements while minimizing the cost for the network operator, subject to the different constraints expressed by the involved actors. This model can be exploited to pursue an initial dimensioning and set-up of the system infrastructure or to dynamically adapt it to support the user security policies. Initial validation shows that allocations generated with our model have considerable advantages in terms of costs and performance compared to traditional approaches.

1 Introduction

In the current Internet, security services are usually active as a set of applications operating at the enterprise border, or through personal protection software installed on the user's personal device. Only recently, network operators are starting to be part of the game, with new service offers coming from major network players. However, when trying to offer security services to a large number of users (potentially tens of million) with current technologies, several limitations are immediately evident. The most important one is the cost of the service, which can be prohibitive, as security services rely mostly on dedicated network appliances, which in turn implies to deploy a huge number of (expensive) middleboxes in different portions of the network. Furthermore, those middleboxes process all the traffic traversing a given link, hence limiting the possibility to offer different services (e.g. parental control to a first user, email content inspection to a second user) to different groups of users.

A possible solution to this problem is offered by the Network Functions Virtualization (NFV) [1] and Software-Defined Networks (SDN) paradigms [2].

© Springer International Publishing Switzerland 2015
F. Cleary and M. Felici (Eds.): CSP Forum 2015, CCIS 530, pp. 65–76, 2015.
DOI: 10.1007/978-3-319-25360-2_6

The former transforms network functions into software appliances, executed in virtual machines on standard high-volume servers, which breaks the tight coupling between hardware and software in existing dedicated (hardware-based) appliances and allows security services to be executed on any server available in the network. The second introduces an unprecedented degree of agility in the network, allowing for a fine (and dynamic) selection of an arbitrary portion of traffic and force it to traverse different network paths. This can be used to give each user the security service he desires, as the traffic of different users can be dynamically redirected to a different set of security appliances.

While this new scenario is definitely appealing, it introduces new challenges as the problem of instantiating and configuring those security services, that are now software applications running in virtual machines (VMs), becomes a multidimensional problem. For instance, in order for a network operator to decide *which* and *where* to install the security services in its network infrastructure, at least the input from three different actors must be taken into consideration (Fig. 1). First, **users** are responsible for the selection of the security services they need (e.g., parental control), as well as the possible definition of some QoS parameter on the service itself and possible preferences with respect to the applications (e.g., use only open source software, use applications from a specific vendor). However, if we consider that future trends show a shift towards "human-friendly" policies (e.g., *"Allow Alice to get Internet access only from 6.00 pm to 9.00 pm"* or *"Block porn and gambling content to my children"*), it becomes immediately clear that the security services requested by each user are not evident from his policies and must be derived automatically by the system, which introduces additional complexity to the problem [3,4].

The second actor is represented by the **developers** of security applications, which need to specify the capabilities of each application and that are required to determine the possible sets of application that can be used to enforce the user policy. In addition, the developer has to specify also application-specific requirements, such as the amount of CPU/memory necessary to achieve a given throughput. Finally, **network operators** are in charge of defining both the network topology and the placement of the servers that will support the execution of the security applications, as well as possible constraints on the network infrastructure (e.g., the traffic of premium users must never traverse congested link, or their applications must be executed on unloaded servers).

This paper provides an initial view of this problem, presenting a preliminary model that, starting from the inputs presented above, can be used to determine the best allocation for the security applications that are needed to satisfy, globally, the requests coming from users while minimizing the cost for the network operator, subject to the different levels of constraints expressed by the involved actors. Particularly, the model aims at providing an answer to the problem of (*a*) **which security applications** are needed, given that several applications may be available for the same task (e.g., content inspection) and that complex services may require the cooperation of several applications; (*b*) **how many instances** of them are required as we can range from having a single instance processing

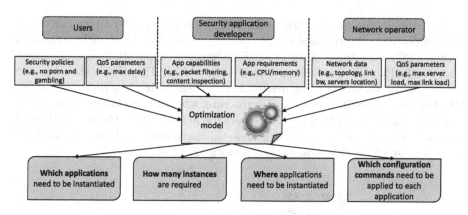

Fig. 1. Model overview.

the traffic of all users to multiple instances each one operating on the traffic of a single user; (c) **where** each instance needs to be allocated, given the resources available in the network; (d) (possibly) **which configuration** commands are needed by each application to provide the requested service.

This model can be exploited either to pursue an initial dimensioning and setup of the system infrastructure or to dynamically adapt it to support the security policies requested by users. In the former case, the network operator can estimate the requests that may come from its users and engineer the network infrastructure in order to minimize its cost, which includes defining hardware and software resources as well as the location of the computing servers in charge of executing the NFV services (and possibly some dedicated hardware appliances, if needed). In the latter (which is left to our future work), the initial dimensioning is coupled with a run-time optimizer that adapts the workload (in terms of applications and their location) on the different computing nodes based on the request coming from the users. The dynamic adaption may provide substantial benefits in presence of nomadic users that require the network to deliver always the same service from different locations (e.g., on the home ADSL when the user is at home or on the 4G network infrastructure when traveling).

This paper is structured as follows. Section 2 presents a small example which highlights the advantages gain by the optimization. Section 3 presents the mathematical model this solution is based on. Section 4 presents the related work. Section 5 summarizes the paper and presents the future work.

2 A Motivating Example

This section presents a motivating example based on the backbone network of a small Internet Service Providers (ISP). The example shows our approach and highlights the advantages, in terms of resources required and execution delay, of the use of an optimization model over the usual (non-optimized) approach when allocating resources to security services.

Let us consider the case where an ISP would like to offer to its customers three different categories of security applications: anti malware (AM), parental control (PC), and traffic filter (TF). Each security application category has a basic (AM_b, PC_b, TF_b) and an advanced version (AM_a, PC_a, TF_a), the advanced version has better security features but is more demanding in terms of resources. The ISP has a tree-like network infrastructure, where the users are connected to the leafs and the root of the tree represents the network core. The non-optimized approach instantiates at each edge node all application and all user-traffic is processed by all applications, as shown in Fig. 2.

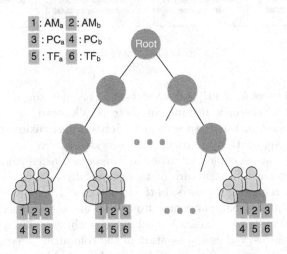

Fig. 2. Non-optimized security applications distribution.

To use our approach and perform the optimization we use more information. The ISP has three different customers types: Fearful, Smart and Unaware. The policies defined by Fearful users are complex and overprotective, consequently several security applications are required to enforce their policies. Smart users define specific policies for only the services that they really need. Unaware users select only the default (basic) security policy. Therefore, not all users require all possible security applications and this is where the optimization occurs.

Our approach considers additional inputs: the distribution of users and their desired security applications, the resource requirements and the execution delay of each security application, and the maximal resources available at each node.

We assume there is a *refinement process* that analyses the user policies and predicts the percentage of security applications required to enforce customers policies. The results of this prediction task for our example are reported in the Table 1. To compute these numbers we assume that every edge node has 100 connected users with a distribution of 30 % Fearful, 20 % Smart and 50 % Unaware.

Table 1. Percentage of users subscribing to a specific service.

		Fearful users	Smart users	Unaware users
Anti-malware	Basic	0 %	40 %	100 %
	Advanced	100 %	60 %	0 %
Parental control	Basic	0 %	0 %	20 %
	Advanced	100 %	40 %	0 %
Traffic filter	Basic	0 %	0 %	0 %
	Advanced	100 %	100 %	0 %

We also assume that each security application can handle the traffic of at most 100 users (which is the same as the non optimized case to allow comparison) and that AM requires four times as much resources as PC, and PC requires four times as much resources as TF. Furthermore the advanced version of a security application requires twice as much resources than the basic version, in formulas:

$$32 \cdot \mathcal{R}(\text{TF}_b) = 16 \cdot \mathcal{R}(\text{TF}_a) = 8 \cdot \mathcal{R}(\text{PC}_b) = 4 \cdot \mathcal{R}(\text{PC}_a) = 2 \cdot \mathcal{R}(\text{AM}_b) = \mathcal{R}(\text{AM}_a)$$

where $\mathcal{R}(x)$ returns the resources needed by the security application x.

The total resources required at the node n_i are given by the sum of all instantiated security applications: $\mathcal{R}_{n_i} = \sum_j^k \mathcal{R}(x_j)$, where x_j are the security applications at n_i. Then, the total resource used to satisfy the policy are $\mathcal{R}_{tot} = \sum_{n_i} \mathcal{R}_{n_i}$.

Figure 3 shows the a security application allocation that satisfy user policies obtained with our optimization model. By comparing it to results in Fig. 2, it is evident that the total number of required security application is reduced, because there are some security applications shared with several users that belong to

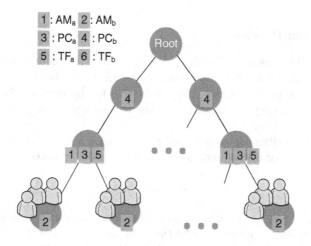

Fig. 3. Optimized security applications distribution.

different edge nodes. Moreover, with our approach, the points of presence where security applications need to be allocated is decreased of 40 %, indeed, in the non-optimized solution $\mathcal{R}_{tot} = 63 \cdot \mathcal{R}(\text{TF}_b) \cdot N$ are needed, while in the optimization solution $\mathcal{R}_{tot} = 37.5 \cdot \mathcal{R}(\text{TF}_b) \cdot N$, where N represents the number of edge nodes.

In addition, our solution has positive impact on the quality of service, because the traffic only passes through the required security applications. For simplicity, we assume that the performance of a security application depends linearly on the number of the users. Therefore, the execution delay introduced by security applications can be computed as $\mathcal{T}_x = \mathcal{T}(x) \cdot \mathcal{N}(x)$ where $\mathcal{T}$ returns the processing time of a security application with a single user and $\mathcal{N}$ returns the number of users that security application. Therefore, the delay experienced by users is computed as $\sum_{x_k} \mathcal{T}_{x_k}$ where x_k are the security applications used by a user.

By also assuming that:

$$4 \cdot \mathcal{T}(\text{TF}_b) = 2 \cdot \mathcal{T}(\text{TF}_a) = 2 \cdot \mathcal{T}(\text{PC}_b) = 2 \cdot \mathcal{T}(\text{AM}_b) = \mathcal{T}(\text{PC}_a) = \mathcal{T}(\text{AM}_a)$$

in our example, the delay added to Smart users is reduced of 60,8 %, Fearful users of 68,7 %, while for Unaware users of 87,7 %, indeed, in the non-optimized solution the delay is $1200 \cdot \mathcal{T}(\text{TF}_b)$ for all users, while with our approach, Smart user delay is $470 \cdot \mathcal{T}(\text{TF}_b)$, Fearful users delay is $376 \cdot \mathcal{T}(\text{TF}_b)$ and Unaware users delay is $148 \cdot \mathcal{T}(\text{TF}_b)$.

3   The Model

In this initial work, we abstract the network as a set of terminal nodes, network nodes, allocation places, and connections. Terminal nodes are nodes where users access the ISP network. Network nodes are generic nodes within the ISP network. Allocation places are network nodes where ISP can setup the security controls needed to satisfy users security requirements (i.e., points of presence).

3.1   Users and Policies

The set with all the users is $U = \{u_i\}$. We name here the security controls to be the security applications (SA) are known: $S = \{\text{SA}_i\}_i$. Without loss of generality we can state that all the policies that can be selected by users are known and in $P = \{p_i\}_i$, e.g., as they are provided by the ISP as a set of predefined security services.

Every user specifies his own policy $P_{u_i} = \{p_i\}_{i<n_i} \subseteq P$ and each policy is associated to a set of SA sequences that can be used to enforce them:

$$\text{sa}(p) = \left\{ (\text{SA}_{1,j}, ..., \text{SA}_{k_i,j})_i \right\}_j$$

where $(\text{SA}_{1,j}, ..., \text{SA}_{k_i,j})_i$ is the i-th policy implementation. A policy implementation is an ordered sequence of SAs that can be used to enforce the policy. In this model, SAs are considered to be chained but the model easily extends to other arrangements that can be modelled as graphs (but it is outside of the scope of this paper).

We assume that all the policy implementations are correct as they are provided by the trusted and correct refinement process. The refinement of all the available policies into sequences of SAs needed to enforce them can be automated or can be manually done by administrators at the network operator. Note that the refinement process also considers possible incompatibilities between SAs when generating the policy implementations.

Moreover, policies are refined in different ways depending on the user due to user preferences, decisions or other limitations. Thus not all the sequences are applicable to all the users (e.g., a user does not want SAs from a specific vendor). Therefore we introduced the following function:

$$sa(p, u_k) = \left\{ (SA_{1,j}, ..., SA_{k_i,j})_i \right\}_j$$

where $sa(p, u_k) \subseteq sa(p)$, that is, user u_k can select only a subset of the available policy implementations.

3.2   SA Instantiation Modes

To further optimize allocation, we consider that SAs can be used in three modes:

- *individual*, when the SA is only used and allocated for a single user;
- *shared*, when the SA is shared among several users. This case is approximated with a single process enforcing a common configuration for all users (single rules can be labelled to be distinguishable). Malicious users can insert rules into the common configuration so that the overall SA performance is affected;
- *multitenant*, when the SA shared among several users but each user has a separate "enforcement engine". This case is approximated with a single coordinating process plus several per-user processes that perform the enforcement. Each per-user process uses a fixed amount of resources. Malicious users cannot affect the performance of other users.

SAs can be used in more than one mode. Shared and multi-tenant can be also used as individual SAs. We do not expect that multi-tenant can also be used as shared ones but we cannot exclude it. The modes are provided in a "SA manifest file" by the application developers.

3.3   Network Model and Allocation

The abstract network allocation model is represented as a graph G:

$$G = ((U \cup N) \cup A, E)$$

Nodes represent the entities: users (in U), network devices (in N), or allocation places (in A). The users are the terminal nodes (i.e., they only have outgoing nodes). Edges in E are only between a node in $(U \cup N)$ and a node in A. Thus G is bipartite.

Allocation places are associated to a set of constraints $\rho(a) = \{c_i\}_{i<m}$ used during the allocation. Examples of constraints are the number of SAs that can be deployed in a given places or relations with the HW resources (e.g., RAM or available CPU cycles). Other constraints are considered during the allocation phase, e.g., shared and multi-tenant should/must not allocated where only a user can be protected.

3.4   Metrics

Taking into account the capabilities and requirements of each security application, specified by its developers, (CPU, memory, throughput, etc.), the metrics can be used to evaluate the impact of the enforcement of a policy on a given SA, they are in the set $M = \{\mu_k\}_k$:

– *SA metrics* that provide a fixed value for each SA, i.e., regardless of the policy and users:
$$\mu_k^f(\text{SA})$$
Examples of these metrics are the cost to buy a SA, the memory size needed to initialize a SA (without configuring anything).
– *policy metrics* that provide a value for each SA-policy pair, i.e., regardless of the users or allocation graph:
$$\mu_k^p(\text{SA}, p)$$
Examples of these metrics are the number of rules to enforce the policy p on SA.
– *policy implementation metrics* whose value depends on the specific user policy implementation and the allocation graph.:
$$\mu_k^i(p, u_i, j)$$
Examples of these metrics use formulas to estimate the overall delay due to the enforcement of a policy p with the policy j-th policy implementation on the abstract allocation graph G.

3.5   Problem Definition

The optimization problem we want to solve is defined as follows:

  "*Given an abstract network allocation model G, a set of users U with their policies $P^{(u_i)}$, their policy implementations* $\text{sa}(p, u_k) = \{(\text{SA}_{1,j}, ..., \text{SA}_{k_i,j})_i\}_j$ *and an optimization function based on the metrics μ_k, find a set of policy implementations that satisfy user policies.*"

We assume there is a function that returns the allocation places that can be used to enforce the j-th policy implementation of user u_k:

$$A(u_k, j) = \{a_1, ...\} \subseteq A$$

This information can be produced during the refinement process. We propose to automatically build an optimization program from the inputs (users, network, policies) based on the selected optimization function. The built optimization problem is then solved using off-the-shelf solvers, as presented in Sect. 3.6.

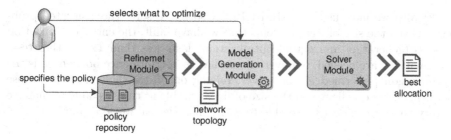

Fig. 4. Prototype architecture.

3.6 Model Implementation: The Prototype

Figure 4 presents the simple linear workflow of the tool. User policies are stored into a repository that is accessed by the Refinement Module. The user is allowed to select from a fixed list of predefined policies. As it is not the main target of this work presented in this paper, current implementation of the Refinement Module is simplified; there is a limited number of policies each one mapped with a fixed function to the SAs that are needed to implement it.

The Model Generation Module reads the mapping of users and security applications and generates the Mixed-integer linear programming (MILP) problem to be optimized by the solver. More in details, this component uses the following inputs when building the optimization problem:

- the target function, which specifies the desired optimization outcome (e.g., the maximization of the network throughput or minimization of the deployment cost);
- the resource limits and the other constraints ρ associated to the current network topology, custom allocations (e.g., Bob's security application must be allocated on node x), which are translated into optimization constraints, mainly inequalities, by the optimization model builder;
- the allocation generation algorithm to use, part of the optimization model builder, which places user implementations $\mathrm{sa}(p, u_k) = \left\{ (\mathrm{SA}_{1,j}, ..., \mathrm{SA}_{k_i,j})_i \right\}_j$ in the valid allocation places for user implementations. Moreover, this algorithm also determines valid allocations by combining an individual allocation for each user. This algorithm does not generate all the possible combinations, but it internally uses metrics to build dominance properties to limit the solution space.
- metric combination functions, which combines metric functions to permit the estimation of the target function for each valid allocation.

We have implemented in our prototype a simple module that generates a linear optimization problem that minimizes the number of used SAs. The optimization model builder has been implemented using a rule engine for complex event processing (Drools [5]).

Finally, we have used the IBM CPLEX solver to solve the generated problems. Given the size of the problems that we have built, the entire optimization process (generation and actual optimization) lasts less than 1 s. Further tests on scalability are needed, however, given that the performance bottleneck is the optimization performed at the solver, relying on off-the-shelf products whose performance is excellent and the size of linear problems that are able to manage is very large, we expect to be able to easily manage real world example.

4   Related Work

Recently, several works have been proposed to adopt NFV and SDN. However, the provisioning of new services by using these paradigms brings up the resource allocation problem. More precisely, in the NFV domain this is known as Virtual Network Function Placement (VNF-P).

An interesting contribution to manage VNF-P is offered by [6]. This work presents and evaluates a formal model for resource allocation within the NFV environments. In particular it considers services that can be allocated on hybrid scenarios, i.e., part of services are instantiated on physical hardware and the others on a virtualized environment. The allocation problem typically has a wide set of solutions, therefore an optimization criteria must be provided to choose among them. Moens et al. propose an Integer Linear Programming (ILP) model to minimize the number of used servers.

Multi-objective Resource Scheduling Algorithm (MORSA) [7] proposes to optimize the resource of the NFV domain by addressing requirements of the infrastructure and the stakeholder policies. In particular, it focuses on the combination of conflicting objectives solving them by using Multi-objective Genetic Algorithm (MOGA). This makes it possible to obtain approximate solutions in a reasonable computation time. The provided architecture follows a plug-in approach that increases the flexibility.

Similarly to the others, Clayman et al. in [8] addresses the dynamic placement of virtualized functions and services. However, this contribution argues that to automatically manage this type of infrastructure a high-level orchestration is needed. In particular, the orchestrator manages the configuration, creation and removal of the virtual nodes and related services. This component is supported by a monitoring system, that collects and reports on the behaviour of the resources.

Beloglazov et al. in [9] propose a strategy to manage live migration (i.e., switching off idles nodes) minimizing power consumption by considering CPU utilization. Finally, García-Valls et al. in [10] describe a graphical discrete event simulation tool for solving the virtual resource allocation in SDN domain.

Gember et al. presented the design, implementation, and evaluation of a network-aware orchestration layer for Middleboxes (MBs), named Stratos [11]. Stratos allows tenants to specify logical middlebox deployments by using a simple logical topology abstraction. The key components of Stratos are an application-aware scheme for scaling, a rack-aware placement and a network-aware flow distribution, which work in concert to carefully manage network resources at various time scales.

Meng et al. in [12] proposed an approach of manipulating VM placement to address the scalability concern in modern data center networks. The authors formulated this problem in a Traffic-aware Virtual Machine Placement Problem (TVMPP), proving its NP-hardness and proposing a two-tier approximation algorithm to solve it efficiently. Another result of this work is an analysis on how traffic patterns and network topology in data centers affect the potential network scalability.

Mehraghdam et al. in [13] have formulated an optimization problem for placing the chained VNF in an operators network with multiple sites, based on requirements of the tenants and the operator. The authors presented a formal model for specifying VNF chaining requests and requirements. In detail an investigation of the possible trade-offs among different optimization objectives with a Pareto set analysis was done.

5 Conclusions and Future Work

This paper presents an initial optimization model capable of selecting the most appropriated security application and determining the best allocation places for them. The model requires as input the number of connected users and their security requirements, all possible allocation places, and the resources available at each allocation place. The resulting deployment configuration has two advantages over a non optimized solution. At first, the deployment cost for a network operator is reduced because less security applications are deployed and therefore less resources are required. Secondly, the quality of the service is improved because less security applications are involved in traffic processing.

Future work will couple the initial dimensioning with a run-time optimizer that adapts the workload on the different computing nodes. The optimization is performed in terms of applications and their locations based on the user demand. This will have substantial benefits in presence of nomadic users, because they require the same services from different locations.

Acknowledgment. The research described in this paper is part of the SECURED project, co-funded by the European Commission (FP7 grant agreement no. 611458).

References

1. The european telecommunications standards institute: network function virtualization - white paper 2. Technical report, October 2013
2. Feamster, N., Rexford, J., Zegura, E.: The road to SDN: an intellectual history of programmable networks. ACM SIGCOMM Comput. Commun. Rev. **44**(2), 87–98 (2014)
3. Basile, C., Lioy, A., Scozzi, S., Vallini, M.: Ontology-based policy translation. In: Herrero, Á., Gastaldo, P., Zunino, R., Corchado, E. (eds.) CISIS 2009. ASC, vol. 63, pp. 117–126. Springer, Heidelberg (2009)

4. Basile, C., Lioy, A., Pitscheider, C., Valenza, F., Vallini, M.: A novel approach for integrating security policy enforcement with dynamic network virtualization. In: NetSoft 2015: 1st IEEE Conference on Network Softwarization, London, UK, April 2014

5. Proctor, M.: Drools: a rule engine for complex event processing. In: Schürr, A., Varró, D., Varró, G. (eds.) AGTIVE 2011. LNCS, vol. 7233, p. 2. Springer, Heidelberg (2012)

6. Moens, H., De Turck, F.: VNF-P: a model for efficient placement of virtualized network functions. In: CNSM 2014: 10th International Conference on Network and Service Management, pp. 418–423, November 2014

7. Yoshida, M., Shen, W., Kawabata, T., Minato, K., Imajuku, W.: MORSA: a multi-objective resource scheduling algorithm for NFV infrastructure. In: APNOMS 2014: 16th Asia-Pacific Network Operations and Management Symposium, pp. 1–6, September 2014

8. Clayman, S., Maini, E., Galis, A., Manzalini, A., Mazzocca, N.: The dynamic placement of virtual network functions. In: NOMS 2014: Network Operations and Management Symposium, pp. 1–9, May 2014

9. Beloglazov, A., Buyya, R.: Energy efficient allocation of virtual machines in cloud data centers. In: CCGrid 2010: 10th IEEE/ACM International Conference on Cluster, Cloud and Grid Computing, pp. 577–578, May 2010

10. García, A.J., Cervelló-Pastor, C., Jiménez, Y.: A modular simulation tool of an orchestrator for allocating virtual resources in SDN. Int. J. Model. Optim. 4(2), 88–99 (2014)

11. Gember, A., Krishnamurthy, A., John, S.S., Grandl, R., Gao, X., Anand, A., Benson, T., Akella, A., Sekar, V.: Stratos: a network-aware orchestration layer for middleboxes in the cloud. CoRR abs/1305.0209, June 2013

12. Meng, X., Pappas, V., Zhang, L.: Improving the scalability of data center networks with traffic-aware virtual machine placement. In: INFOCOM 2010, San Diego, CA, pp. 1–9, March 2010

13. Mehraghdam, S., Keller, M., Karl, H.: Specifying and placing chains of virtual network functions. In: CloudNet 2014: IEEE 3rd International Conference on Cloud Networking, Luxembourg, pp. 7–13, October 2014

Risk and Trust

Medusa: A Supply Chain
Risk Assessment Methodology

Nineta Polemi and Panayiotis Kotzanikolaou[✉]

Department of Informatics, University of Piraeus,
Greece 80 Karaoli Dimitriou Street, 18534 Piraeus, Greece
{dpolemi,pkotzani}@unipi.gr

Abstract. Although efforts have been made to standardize Supply Chain (SC) security risk assessment, there is a lack of targeted methodologies. In this paper we propose Medusa, a SC risk assessment methodology, compliant with ISO28001. Medusa can be used in order to assess the overall risk of the entire supply chain. The derived overall risk values are used in order to generate a *baseline SC security policy,* identifying the least necessary security controls for each participant in the SC. In addition, Medusa assesses the risk of cascading threat scenarios within a SC. This enables the SC participants to fine-tune their security policies according to their business role as well as their dependencies.

Keywords: Supply chain · Risk assessment · Critical Infrastructures · Dependency graphs

1 Introduction

For over a decade significant research efforts have been made towards risk assessment methodologies especially suited to Critical Infrastructures (CIs). In principle, most of the risk assessment methodologies focus on the identification of threats, vulnerabilities and the related impact and ultimately on the evaluation of the underlying risks. However, most risk assessment methodologies are organization-oriented and do not consider the cascading effects occurring from cross-sectoral and/or cross-border dependencies. As a consequence, they tend to focus on organization-wide risks and they fail to capture the security needs of more complex eco-systems of interdependent organizations. Supply chains (SC) are instances of complex, inter-dependent eco-systems. SC security management involves the assessment of security risks deriving from interdependent CIs from various sectors, with the transportation sector playing a central role.

According to the ISO 28001 standard on security management systems for the supply chain [11], a SC is the set of resources and processes which begins with the provision of raw materials and extends through the delivery of products or services to the customer through the different transport means. Obviously, there is a need for extending and validating existing risk assessment frameworks in terms of their ability to deal with SC risk assessment, including the dependencies associated with the provisioning of the SC services. A starting point for modeling cascading effects lies in the understanding of the interdependencies of the various infrastructures [14, 17] which include physical, cyber, geographic and other (logical dependencies).

© Springer International Publishing Switzerland 2015
F. Cleary and M. Felici (Eds.): CSP Forum 2015, CCIS 530, pp. 79–90, 2015.
DOI: 10.1007/978-3-319-25360-2_7

In this paper we present Medusa, a risk assessment methodology that aims to systematically evaluate the security risks affecting CI operators[1] within a SC. The goal of Medusa is twofold. First, to assess the overall security risks of a SC. The derived overall risk values are used in order to define a baseline SC security policy, defining the least necessary security controls required by each business partner. Emphasis has been given in ensuring the compliance with relative security standards [9–11]. In addition, Medusa allows the risk assessor to assess the risk of cascading threat scenarios which may be realized within a SC. The study of the cascading scenarios takes into consideration the graph relations of a potential source of a threat as well as the business role of each participant by utilizing weights of business importance. Medusa enables all the SC participants to fine-tune their security policies according to their business role in the examined SC. This paper is organized as follows: In Sect. 2, existing risk assessment methodologies are overviewed from the scope of their appropriateness in addressing SC security needs. Section 3 presents the Medusa risk assessment methodology. Section 4 concludes this paper and describes future work.

2 Research Efforts Towards Supply Chain Risk Assessment

Risk management international standards range from general considerations and guidelines for risk management processes (*e.g.* [7, 8]), to specific guidelines for the IT sector (*e.g.* [9, 10]), and to CI dependency analysis risk assessment methodologies (*e.g.* [1, 2, 4–6, 13, 18, 19]), all the way to sector specific frameworks as, for example, in the maritime sector (*e.g.*, [14, 15]). Most of these standards specify framework conditions for the risk management process, but do not provide specific methodologies targeted to SC risk assessment. In principle, choosing the right method and tool for risk assessment proves to be complicated. Since SCs are originating from a business context, SC risk management methods are usually quantitative and are based on monetary costs or potential impact (*e.g.* [3, 10, 16]). In practice, the selection of a specific risk-assessment tool is based on practical considerations, and depends on how well the present terminology of the application can be mapped onto the predefined specific terminology of the risk assessment methodology.

Security and risk management in the transportation sector (a key sector for SC management) emphasizes on safety. For example, the International Ship and Port Facility Security (ISPS) Code (as well as the respective EU regulation EC725/2004) defines a set of measures to enhance the physical security of port facilities and ships. Methodologies for security assessment are described and a guideline for the implementation of the respective security measures is given. Additionally, roles and responsibilities concerning maritime security at various levels are defined. Nevertheless, due to the increased interaction and exchange of information of ports with other CIs in the maritime eco-system (*e.g.* port authorities, ministries, maritime companies, ship industry, etc.) the sole focus on physical security is not sufficient and the security of the port's ICT systems becomes equally important.

---

[1] Following the ISO 28001 standard, we will call such operators as *business partners*.

ISO 28001 [11] is the security management standard specifically developed for SC, due to an increased demand from the transportation and logistics industry. It specifies the requirements for a SC security management system, including aspects related to financing, manufacturing, information management and the facilities for packing, storing and transferring goods between modes of transport and locations. ISO 28001 is applicable to all sizes of organizations in manufacturing, service, storage or transportation at any stage of the SC. The standard defines the need for certification by an accredited third party and/or a self-declaration of conformance with the standard. ISO 28001 describes a generic methodology and provides a generic guideline for organizations seeking to implement or refine a specific methodology. Finally, NISTIR 7622 [12] aims to provide a notional set of SC assurance methods and practices that offer a SC security management for federal information systems. Although in [12] the need for a SC risk management methodology is recognized, the document itself does not define such a methodology.

3 The Medusa Risk Assessment Supply Chain Methodology

The main design criteria of the Medusa SC risk assessment methodology are:

- *Holistic View*: Medusa aims to provide a holistic SC view in order to identify global SC threats, such as the *cascading threats* within the SC. These may not always be easy to identify from an organization-centric perspective.
- *Collaborative*: Medusa aims to promote collaboration between business partners.
- *Compliance with Standards*: Medusa will be compliant with a range of existing standards such as [9–11], as a means of increasing its adoption and longevity.

3.1 Notation and Concepts

Medusa SC risk assessment relies on *SC dependency graphs*, used to visualize the dependencies within a SC (see Fig. 1 for an example of a SC Graph):

1. *Supply Chain Graph*. A directed graph $SCG = (\mathbb{N}, \mathcal{E})$ where $\mathbb{N}$ is the set nodes and ε is the set of edges.
   (a) Node $x_i \in \mathbb{N}$. It represents a business partner participating in a supply chain.
   (b) Directed edge $x_i \rightarrow x_j \in \mathcal{E}$. It represents a service provided by x_i to x_j in order to support the provisioning of the SC services.
2. *Weight of x_i (w_i)*: The importance of x_i for the provisioning of the SC service. It represents *the business impact* of a business partner (node) for the provisioning of the SC service. The following scale is used:
   (a) $w(x_i) = 1$ (*High*) if its absence/disruption of its operations results to severe delay/disruption of the provisioning of the service provided by the SC.
   (b) $w(x_i) = 0.5$ (*Medium*) if its absence/disruption of its operations results to important delay/disruption of the provisioning of the service provided by the SC.
   (c) $w(x_i) = 0.25$ (*Low*) if its absence/disruption of its operations results to limited delay/disruption of the provisioning of the service provided by the supply SC.

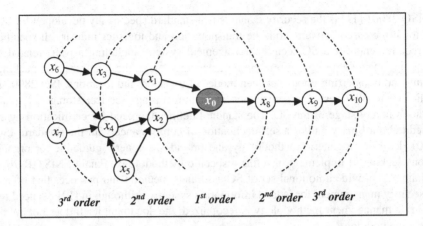

Fig. 1. An example of a SC Graph. Order defined with respect to the node x_0 (either as source or as destination node).

3. $order(x_i, x_j)$: The order of a business partner x_j in relation to another business partner x_i is defined as the number of steps required for x_i to reach x_j using the smallest length (shortest) path: $order(x_i, x_j) = \min(\{|\text{path}(x_i, x_j)|\})$.

For example in Fig. 1 we have, $order(x_0, x_8) = 1$ and $order(x_5, x_0) = 2$.

3.2   The Methodology

Step 0: Scope of the SC Risk Assessment. Initially, the risk assessor (in consensus with the business partners) will define a *Statement of Application* that describes the scope, the goal and the outcome of the *SC Service* (SCS) under examination. The risk assessor may create use-cases to clarify the business processes of the SCS.

Step 1: Analysis of the SCS. The SCS, defined in Step 0, is decomposed as follows:

1. *Create a SCS Graph*

Business process modeling of the SCS is based on Supply Chain Graphs (SCG), defined in Sect. 3.1. The business partners will provide input related with their business role and dependencies within the SCS. By using this input, the assessor will design the SCG corresponding to the SCS (as shown in Fig. 1).

2. *Business Partners Declaration Statements*

In this step, all business partners will provide their *Security Declaration Statements* as defined in ISO28001 [11]. An example is shown in Table 1. Medusa extends ISO28001 in two ways: (a) it assigns each security control defined in the declaration with a unique id, to be used in the following steps of the methodology, and (b) it allows business partners to declare *partial implementation* of controls.

Table 1. (Part of) A Security Declaration Statement (Available at: http://athina.cs.unipi.gr/medusa/index.php).

Implementation Level Factor (Security Controls)	Yes	No	Partially	Comments
(1) Management of Supply Chain Security				
$C_{1.1}$ Does the organization have a management system that addresses supply chain security?				
$C_{1.2}$ Does the organization have a person designated as responsible for supply chain security?				

Step 2: SC-Threat Identification. Threat identification will be derived from the model produced in Step 1. In particular:

1. Adopt a Threat Categorization

Threats related with SC services usually involve complex threat scenarios affecting multiple partners, rather than small-scale threats affecting a single organization. Threat categorization will allow the effective mapping of threat categories to a subset of security controls. Medusa uses four threat categories, shown in Table 2.

2. Define Threat Scenarios for Each Threat Category

For each threat category defined in step 2.1, specific threat scenarios that are relevant to SC services are identified. At least the threat scenarios defined in [11] should be

Table 2. Mapping threat categories to specific threat scenarios and to required security controls. All security controls are defined in the Security Declaration Statement.

Threat Category	Threat Scenarios	Required Security Controls
TC-1: Infrastructural Threats.	$TS_{1.1}$: Destroy a major / critical SC Infrastructure $TS_{1.2}$: Suspected or confirmed unauthorized access to SC Infrastructures	$C_{1.1}$, $C_{1.2}$ $C_{2.1}$, $C_{2.2}$, $C_{2.3}$ $C_{3.1}$, $C_{3.2}$, $C_{3.3}$, $C_{3.4}$ $C_{6.1}$, $C_{6.2}$
TC-2: Information & ICT Threats	$TS_{2.1}$: Information tampering $TS_{2.2}$: Information loss $TS_{2.3}$: Communication interruption or loss $TS_{2.4}$: Software/system abuse	$C_{1.1}$, $C_{1.2}$ $C_{2.1}$, $C_{2.2}$, $C_{2.3}$ $C_{5.1}$, $C_{5.2}$, $C_{5.3}$, $C_{5.4}$, $C_{5.5}$, $C_{5.6}$, $C_{5.7}$
TC-3: Personnel Security and Safety	$TS_{3.1}$: People under attack $TS_{3.2}$: Misuse / abuse of SC procedures	$C_{1.1}$, $C_{1.2}$, $C_{2.1}$, $C_{2.2}$, $C_{2.3}$ $C_{4.1}$, $C_{4.2}$, $C_{4.3}$, $C_{4.4}$
TC-4: Goods and Conveyance Security	$TS_{4.1}$: Intrude and/or take control of an asset (including conveyances) within the supply chain. $TS_{4.2}$: Use the supply chain as a means of smuggling. $TS_{4.3}$: Cargo Integrity $TS_{4.4}$: Unauthorized use $TS_{4.5}$: Goods and Conveyance misuse	$C_{1.1}$, $C_{1.2}$ $C_{2.1}$, $C_{2.2}$, $C_{2.3}$ $C_{3.1}$, $C_{3.2}$, $C_{3.3}$, $C_{3.4}$, $C_{3.5}$ $C_{6.1}$, $C_{6.2}$, $C_{6.3}$, $C_{6.4}$, $C_{6.5}$ $C_{7.1}$, $C_{7.2}$, $C_{7.3}$, $C_{7.4}$

examined. Medusa defines an extended set of threat scenarios for each category (see Table 2). The assessor may also examine additional threats.

3. *Define Security Requirements for Each Threat Category*

The threat categories defined in step 2.1, and consequently the specific threat scenarios defined in step 2.2, are now mapped to the security controls, as defined in the Security Declaration Statements (see Table 2).

Step 3: Assess Expected Likelihood for Possible Threat Scenarios. In this Step, the expected likelihood for each possible threat scenario for the SCS will be estimated. The likelihood of each TS will take into consideration two values: a threat level, reflecting the probability of occurrence, and a vulnerability level, reflecting the current level of implementation of the relative security controls for each business partner.

1. *Threat Assessment*

The probability of occurrence for each possible threat scenario is defined as the expected frequency of appearance (*e.g.* in the range [0-100 %]) of the threat scenario being realized, in the SCS under examination. Let $t_i(TS_j)$ denote the probability of a particular threat scenario TS_j being realized, as assessed by the business partner x_i.

2. *Vulnerability Assessment*

Lack of security controls for a threat scenario will lead to a high vulnerability of against this particular threat scenario. Vulnerability assessment will make use of the Security Declaration Statements completed by each business partner (see Table 1), where each business partner has provided information related with the implementation level of security controls related with the SC. In addition, the mapping of the Threat Categories (and consequently of Threat Scenarios) to the required security controls as described in Table 2, can be combined to provide a complete view of the level of implementation of the security controls for each examined threat.

Table 3 shows an example of a vulnerability assessment table. Based on the score of each business partner, the vulnerability level of each business partner is estimated as follows: Let $v_i(TS_j)$ denote the vulnerability level of x_i for a threat scenario TS_j. The value $v_i(TS_j)$ is computed as follows. For each threat, let $Impl_{max}(TS_j)$ denote the maximum possible implementation score that a business partner would get, if *all* the proposed controls for this threat were fully implemented. Let $Impl_i(TS_j)$ denote the implementation score of the business partner x_i for the threat scenario TS_j as computed based on Table 3. Then the vulnerability level of the business partner x_i for the threat scenario TS_j is computed as:

$$v_i(TS_j) = \left[1 - \frac{Impl_i(TS_j)}{Impl_{max}(TS_j)}\right] \times 100 \qquad (1)$$

Table 3. Mapping threats to related security controls and implementation levels

TS$_{11}$: Destroy a major /critical SC Infrastructure

Related Security Controls	Level of Implementation (Yes = 2, Partially = 1, No = 0)			
	x_o	x_1	...	x_n
$C_{1.1}$ Does the organization have a management system that addresses supply chain security?	2	1	...	1
$C_{1.2}$ Does the organization have a person designated as responsible for supply chain security?	0	1	...	2
$C_{2.1}$ Does the organization have (a) current security plan(s)?	2	1	...	1
...	...	...	...	...
$C_{6.2}$ Are qualified persons designated to supervise cargo operations?				
Implementation Score: $Imp_i(TS_j)$				

3. Likelihood Assessment

The likelihood assessment for each examined threat scenario is computed as the product of the relative threat and vulnerability values. The likelihood of occurrence of a Threat Scenario TS_j to a business partner x_i is computed as:

$$l_i(TS_j) = t_i(TS_j) \times v_i(TS_j) \tag{2}$$

Step 4: Assess the Consequence for Each Threat Scenario. Each business partner will be assessed for its expected consequence, as defined in [11], if a threat scenario were realized.

1. Define a Consequence Classification

We extend the classification of consequence described in [11] and we propose the classification shown in Table 4.

2. Consequence Assessment

For each examined threat scenario, the consequence of each business partner is assessed (for the SC Service under examination). The values are in the range [0–100], following the classification of Table 4. Let $c_i(TS_j)$ denote the consequence experienced by the business partner x_i by a threat scenario TS_j being realized.

Step 5: Assess the Risk for Each Examined Threat Scenario. In this Step, the expected security risk for each possible threat scenario is assessed.

- The *partial risk level* of the business partner x_i for the examined threat scenario TS_j is calculated as: $r(TSj) = li(TSj) \times ci(TSj)$.
- The *overall risk level*, involving all business partners in the SC is calculated as:
- $R(TS_j) = max(\{r_i(TS_j)\}), \forall x_i \in \mathbb{N}$.

Table 4. Classification of consequence

Classification		Description of the Consequence Level
Rating	Value	
High	(70–100]	*Death & Injury* – loss of life on a certain scale, and/or
		Economic Impact – major damage to a asset and/or infrastructure preventing further operations, and/or
		Environmental Impact – complete destruction of multiple aspects of the ecosystem over a large area, and/or
		Cascading impact – severe damages will cascade to at least one business partner within the SC
Medium	(30–70]	*Death & Injury* – loss of life, and/or
		Economic Impact – damage to asset and/or infrastructure requiring repairs, and/or
		Environmental Impact – long term damage to a portion of the ecosystem, and/or
		Cascading impact – some damages will cascade to the SC
Low	[0–30]	*Death & Injury* – injuries but no loss of life, and/or
		Economic Impact – minimal damage to a asset and/or infrastructure and systems, and/or
		Environmental Impact – some environmental damage

Step 6: Assess the Risk of Cascading Threats for Each Examined Threat Scenario. In this Step, the risk assessor will make use of all the risk parameters computed in the previous steps, in order to evaluate the effect of potential cascading threats for each examined threat scenario. The risk assessment of cascading threats is based on the methodology proposed in [13].

1. *Assess the Risk of Cascading Dependencies Within the SC-Graph*

In order to analyze cascading threat scenarios, first all possible cascading paths are defined, based on the dependencies between the business partners. Then, the expected dependency risk of each examined dependency chain for each examined threat scenario is computed, based on the following algorithm:

1. Define a minimum and a maximum path length ℓ_{min} and ℓ_{max} respectively. Typical values are dependency paths between 2 to 5 nodes.
2. Each node within the SCG will be examined as a potential initiator of a cascading chain. Without loss of generality, say that y_0 is the source node of a chain.
3. For each examined source node y_0, identify all possible dependency chains that initiate from y_0 with length between ℓ_{min} and ℓ_{max}. Without loss of generality, say that $y_0 \rightarrow y_1 \rightarrow \ldots y_n$ is one dependency chain initiating from the node y_0.
4. For each identified dependency chain, use the following steps to assess the risk of the dependency chain.
   (a) For each threat scenario TS_j:
      (i) For each node acting as a source node y_0:

(1) For each dependency chain $y_0 \rightarrow y_1 \rightarrow \ldots y_n$ initiating from y_0 (with length between ℓ_{min} and ℓ_{max}), compute the cumulative *cascading dependency risk* $R_{01\ldots n}(TS_j)$ as:

$$R_{01\ldots n}(TS_j) = \sum_{i=0}^{n} \left(\prod_{k=0}^{i} l_k(TS_j) \right) \cdot w_i(TS_j) \cdot c_i(TS_j) \tag{3}$$

2. Rank Threats Scenarios According to the Cascading Dependency Risk Values

Using the cumulative cascading dependency risk values, all the cumulative cascading dependency risk values for all threat scenarios and all possible chains are ranked in descending order. This ranking will provide input for the prioritization of the required security controls.

Step 7: Selection of Appropriate Security Controls. In this Step, security controls are selected for the business partners participating in the SC Service under examination, based on the risk assessment results.

1. *Setting Risk Thresholds*

   (a) Let $\mathcal{R}$ denote the maximum acceptable *risk threshold* for the SCS. The goal will be to reduce the risk level $r_i(TS_j)$ of every business partner (and consequently $R(TS_j)$) below the risk threshold, by applying additional security controls.

   (b) Let $\mathcal{RC}$ denote the maximum acceptable *cascading risk threshold*. The goal will be to reduce the risk level of every cascading dependency risk $R_{01\ldots n}(TS_j)$ below $\mathcal{RC}$, by applying additional security controls to specific business partners.

2. *Required Security Controls for the SC*

   (a) For each threat scenario TS_j, check $R(TS_j)$.

      (i) If $R(TS_j) \leq \mathcal{R}$, then no additional security controls are required.

      (ii) If $R(TS_j) > R$, then use the ranked risk values, to identify which business partners exhibit partial risk values $r_i(TS_j) > R$. These business partners will be required to apply additional security controls.

      (iii) Examine cumulative cascading risk values.

         (1) If $R_{01\ldots n}(TS_j) > RC$, then by using the ranked cascading dependency risk values, identify which business partners are potential initiators of dependency chains with dependency risk higher that $\mathcal{RC}$. These nodes should be treated with the highest priority in order to reduce their dependency risk bellow the risk threshold.

   (b) Repeat until all risks/dependency risks are bellow their threshold ($\mathcal{R} or \mathcal{RC}$).

3.3 Example: Examining "Vehicles' Transport" Supply Chain

We will use the *purchase & shipment* SC sub process of the "vehicles transport service", to briefly describe a test scenario for the Medusa methodology. The *Importer* initiates the SC by sending a purchase order to the *Industry* for a number of vehicles. Once both have agreed upon the terms of the contract (pricing, documentation, freight charges, currency etc.), the Industry contracts a *Ship Agent* to deliver the vehicles to the destination port. The *Ship Agent* makes the arrangements with the *Ship Owner* to assure usage of ships; with *Customs Authorities* to arrange for the Manifest Registration Number; with the departure *Port Authority* to arrange the ship formalities related to the authorization process from the entry of the ship into the port until its exit and then proceed to load the vehicles into the vessel for shipment to the destination port. The Ship Agent contracts a *Vehicle Transport Agent* and assigns the transfer of the vehicles from the Industry to the departure Port. Finally, the Ship Agent sends the relevant documentation to the Importer's *Local Agent* who has the responsibility for the ship arrival and the regional procedure of delivering the vessel to the importer. Figure 2 shows the SCG representing the dependencies between all the above entities (cyber or physical ones).

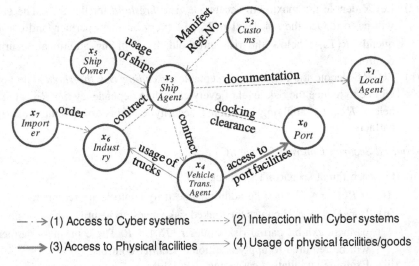

Fig. 2. A SCG based on the dependencies of the *purchase & shipment* SC

We examine the threat scenario $TS_{1.1}$ (Destroy a major/critical SC Infrastructure). Assuming that the threat and consequence values shown in Table 5 were provided by each business partner and that the vulnerability values were computed by applying Eq. (1) on the input provided by the Security Declaration Statement of each partner, then the partial and overall risk values for this threat scenario are calculated. In order to assess the threat level, each partner considers the possiblility of occurance either to the partner itself, or to someone else due to their dependence. For example, the Port (x_0) considers itself as the target of he threat, while the Vehicle Transfer Agent (x_4)

considers the possibility of being used as a threat agent against the Port infrastructure. Very low threat values bellow a threshold (say ≤ 5 %) are not considered. This is reasonable to expect since not all business partners are subject to the same threats. Now Eq. (3) can be applied to compute all the possible cascading dependency risks for all possible dependency paths, to prioritize risk mitigation.

Table 5. Summarizing the assessment of the partial and overall risk values

	Business partners involved in the SC							
	x_0	x_1	x_2	x_3	x_4	x_5	x_6	x_7
$t_i(TS_j) \times$	30%	-	-	-	20%	10%	-	-
$v_i(TS_j) =$	20				40	10		
$l_i(TS_j) \times$	6%				8%	1%		
$c_i(TS_j) =$	75				25	10			$R(TS_{1.1})$
$r_i(TS_j)$	4,5				2	1			4,5

4 Conclusions and Future Work

Medusa attempts to cover two main goals: First to be a practical SC risk assessment methodology fully compliant with ISO28001. In addition, Medusa aims to also capture and assess the cascading risks within the supply chain. Towards this direction, Medusa extends ISO28001 in several ways. First it defines threat categories and uses them to group specific threat scenarios. Then the threat categories are mapped to specific subsets of the security controls already defined in the Security Declaration Statements. Thus by using the Statements provided by all business partners, it is easy to quantify the vulnerability (and eventually likelihood) of each partner for each examined threat scenario. In addition Medusa allows the efficient assessment of cascading risks within the SC; by using input data already provided in the previous steps, all potential dependency chains of the SC are assessed and their cascading risk values are then used to prioritize risk mitigation. Currently we are working under the Medusa project, on developing a collaborative tool to fully implement the proposed methodology, and to validate its results using actual operators of supply chains.

Acknowledgements.   The publication of this paper has been partly supported by the University of Piraeus Research Center. – This work is supported by the European Commission under grant agreement HOME/2013/CIPS/AG/4000005093 (MEDUSA: http://medusa.cs.unipi.gr/).

References

1. Aung, Z.Z., Watanabe, K.: A framework for modeling interdependencies in Japan's critical infrastructures. In: Palmer, C., Shenoi, S. (eds.): 3rd IFIP International Conferenceon Critical Infrastructure Protection (CIP-2009), pp. 243–257. Springer, USA (2009)

2. De Porcellinis, S., Oliva, G., Panzieri, S., Setola, R.: A holistic-reductionistic approach for modeling interdependencies. In Palmer, C., Shenoi, S. (eds.): 3rd IFIP International Conference on Critical Infrastructure Protection (CIP-2009), pp. 215–227, Springer, USA (2009)
3. Giannopoulos, G., Filippini, R., Schimmer, M.: Risk assessment methodologies for Critical Infrastructure Protection. Part I: A state of the art. Joint Research Center Publication, JRC 70046, EUR 25286 EN, ISBN 978-92-79-23839-0, ISSN 1831-9424, doi: 10.2788/22260. Publications Office of the European Union, Luxembourg (2012)
4. Haimes, Y., Santos, J., Crowther, K., Henry, M., Lia, N.C., Yan, Z.: Risk analysis in interdependent infrastructures. Crit. Infrastruct. Prot. **253**, 297–310 (2007)
5. Hokstad, P., Utne, I.B., Vatn, J. (eds.): Risk and interdependencies in critical infrastructures. A Guideline for Analysis. In: Springer Series in Reliability Engineering VIII, 252 (2013)
6. ISO, ISO 31000: Risk Management – Principles and Guidelines. Geneva (2009)
7. ISO, ISO 31010: Risk management – Risk assessment techniques. Geneva (2009)
8. ISO, ISO 27001: Information Security Management System Requirements. Geneva, Switzerland (2013)
9. ISO, ISO 27005: Information security risk management, Geneva (2011)
10. ISO, ISO 28001: Security management systems for the supply chain — Best practices for implementing supply chain security, assessments and plans — Requirements and guidance. Geneva, Switzerland (2007)
11. Kotzanikolaou, P., Theoharidou, M., Gritzalis, D.: Assessing n-order dependencies between critical infrastructures. Int. J. Crit. Infrastruct. **9**(1/2), 93–110 (2013)
12. NIST, Notional Supply Chain Risk Management Practices for Federal Information Systems. http://nvlpubs.nist.gov/nistpubs/ir/2012/NIST.IR.7622.pdf
13. Ntouskas, T., Polemi, N.: Collaborative security management services for port information systems. In: DCNET/ICE-B/OPTICS, pp. 305–308 (2012)
14. Pederson, P., Dudenhoeffer, D., Hartley, S., Permann, M.: Critical Infrastructure Interdependency Modeling: A Survey of U.S. and International Research, INL, INL/EXT-06-11464 (2006)
15. Peltier, T.R.: Information security risk analysis. Auerbach Publications, Boston (2001)
16. Polemi, N., Ntouskas, T.: Open issues and proposals in the it security management of commercial ports: the S-PORT national case. In: Gritzalis, D., Furnell, S., Theoharidou, M. (eds.) SEC 2012. IFIP AICT, vol. 376, pp. 567–572. Springer, Heidelberg (2012)
17. Rinaldi, S.M., Peerenboom, J.P., Kelly, T.K.: Identifying, understanding and analyzing critical infrastructure interdependencies. IEEE Control Syst. **21**, 11–25 (2001)
18. Theoharidou, M., Kotzanikolaou, P., Gritzalis, D.: Risk assessment methodology for interdependent critical infrastructures. Int. J. Risk Assess. Manage. **15**(2/3), 128–148 (2011)
19. Zio, E., Sansavini, G.: Modeling interdependent network systems for identifying cascade-safe operating margins interdependency. IEEE Trans. Reliab. **60**(1), 94–101 (2011)

Evidence-Based Trustworthiness of Internet-Based Services Through Controlled Software Development

Francesco Di Cerbo[1], Nazila Gol Mohammadi[2], and Sachar Paulus[3](✉)

[1] SAP Product Security Research, Mougins, France
francesco.di.cerbo@sap.com
[2] Paluno - The Ruhr Institute for Software Technology,
University of Duisburg-Essen, Duisburg, Germany
nazila.golmohammadi@paluno.uni-due.de
[3] Mannheim University of Applied Sciences, Mannheim, Germany
s.paulus@hs-mannheim.de

Abstract. Users of Internet-based services are increasingly concerned about the trustworthiness of these services (i.e., apps, software, platforms) thus slowing down their adoption. Therefore, successful software development processes have to address trust concerns from the very early stages of development using constructive and practical methods to enable the trustworthiness of software and services. Unfortunately, even well-established development methodologies do not specifically support the realization of trustworthy Internet-based services today, and trustworthiness-oriented practices do not take objective evidences into account. We propose to use controlled software life-cycle processes for trustworthy Internet-based services. Development, deployment and operations processes, can be controlled by the collection of trustworthiness evidences at different stages. This can be achieved by e.g., measuring the degree of trustworthiness-related properties of the software, and documenting these evidences using digital trustworthiness certificates. This way, other stakeholders are able to verify the trustworthiness properties in a later stages, e.g., in the deployment of software on a marketplace, or the operation of the service at run-time.

Keywords: Trust · Trustworthiness · Software Development Methodology · Digital Trustworthiness Certificate · Metrics · Evidences

1 Introduction

The adoption and acceptance of Internet-based services by the end-users are largely dependent on whether users have trust into these services. [15]. Security and trustworthiness have become more critical because of *(a)* ubiquity of the Internet makes it difficult to produce secure software in the first place, *(b)* the increasing general distrust into the Internet (e.g., related to Snowden's revelations[1]). Existing software life-cycle processes and approaches were not able to

---

[1] See http://www.theguardian.com/us-news/the-nsa-files for an overview.

© Springer International Publishing Switzerland 2015
F. Cleary and M. Felici (Eds.): CSP Forum 2015, CCIS 530, pp. 91–102, 2015.
DOI: 10.1007/978-3-319-25360-2_8

successfully address this important requirement. Despite different theoretic (e.g., automated proving, data flow analysis techniques etc.) and practical (Common Criteria [10], Microsoft SDL [25] etc.) approaches, we still often see that software either is not able to be (or stay) secure, or that it is not used for potential trust reasons, or both. The authors believe that the current software development and operations approaches need some improvement in order to successfully address the complex issue of delivering trustworthy services. The major development practices towards trustworthiness used today are either too limiting and constrained (leading to a very complex and costly process) or too much based on the individual competences of the people working on the software (where the quality and trustworthiness of the software/services is difficult to manage). In case of being too constrained, it would actually impact usage, usability or simple development efforts negatively. In the other case, with a too "loose" methodology, it will be with high probability vulnerable and less aligned with the necessary goals and elements towards trustworthiness.

Proposal Overview. This paper proposes a new type of approach towards developing, deploying and operating trustworthy Internet-based services. The basic idea is to create a trade-off between the formal, *constrained* approach and the rather informal, *uncontrolled* approach. Hence, we aim at a *controlled* approach, similar to the introduction of software quality in general, but in our case adjusted to the requirements of trustworthy software and (Internet-based) services.

A new stiff development process will therefore not be successful at a large scale (one of the drawbacks of Common Criteria is that it mandates a certain development model which in practice typically leads to run the development process twice: *(1)* for the software, and *(2)* for the required documentation for the certification), due to the existing variety and fragmentation of development practices and methodologies. To introduce some sort of control during the software development process, we therefore need to be development process agnostic. Moreover, since the trustworthiness of software and Internet-based services can be highly impacted during deployment and operations, the approach must take the full life-cycle of the software into account.

We introduce measurements and thus evidence collection in different phases of the software life-cycle, e.g., metric values that express the degree of fulfilment of trustworthiness properties. They allow some sort of *prediction* of the to-be-expected trustworthiness properties, and thus to steer and manage development activities and correspondingly focus and financial investments towards the trustworthiness goals. The trustworthiness evidences can be applied to any development process model, and may be used to evaluate the usefulness of trustworthiness-enabling capability patterns [19] as best practice elements (e.g., threat modelling, data flow analysis, user experience design etc.). It is, though, important that the evidences fulfil a number of conditions so that they can be successfully used. For details, see Sect. 4. We use the digital trustworthiness certificates to express trustworthiness properties in a verifiable manner that also cater assertions on the observed evidences. This allows to propagate trustworthiness evidences to subsequent phases of the software life-cycle like in software provisioning, e.g., in a marketplace, the values of the trustworthiness metrics may serve as input for a decision support system for selecting solutions [5]. To sum up, any software life-cycle methodology can be enriched by an evidence approach (identification of trustworthiness qualities, definition of metrics and measurement procedures, evidence collection and interpretation) to make the trustworthiness of the developed software manageable and controllable. Quantitative and qualitative trustworthiness assertions expressed in digital trustworthiness certificates allow to propagate this control to other parts of the software life-cycle.

To facilitate the acceptance of proposed approach, a light-weight certification scheme is developed where, the deployment and operation of an Internet-based service can receive a certification based on the evidenced and used digital trustworthiness certificates. This process is light-weight, since it does not require any additional development-related activity if our approach is used. The only remaining additional step is a validation of the (quantitative or qualitative) assertions in the digital trustworthiness certificates by an independent body. To achieve a fast market adoption, a self-validation may be an option as well.

The remainder of this paper is organized as follows: Sect. 2 provides a brief overview on the fundamental concepts and related work with respect to addressing trustworthiness. In Sect. 3, we propose different categories of development methodologies, and in Sect. 4 we describe the elements necessary for our approach. Section 5 presents our solution in the context of different application scenarios. Section 6 concludes the paper and an gives outlook on future work, including a potential process certification for demonstrating the successful application of the overall approach to a software product or Internet-based service.

2   Background and Related Work

This section summarizes the result of our analysis on existing software development methodologies in buliding trustworthiness into software. A brief overview of development methodologies can be found in our previous work [24]. Although, it does not specify how these methodologies contribute to the trustworthiness of the end-product. There, we did not aim on providing solution to extend these methodologies in enabling trustworthiness.

There are many research contributions towards constructive quality assurance of software systems, proposing guidelines, principles, and methodologies for developing high-quality software. There are also more generic and well-established development methodologies that can be tuned into more security-aware variants, and there are specialized constrained methodologies that are probably not relevant for most organizations. Sommerville [28] states that reuse-oriented, or test-driven development can, in principle, result in trustworthy systems as well, since continuous user feedback, reuse, and early testing can enhance software quality and mitigate risks. Eliciting end-user requirement is a key aspect of User-Centered Design [29], which can be seen as potential to consider user s trust concerns early in the development. Weigert [32] conclude that model-driven engineering [26] significantly facilitates the development of trustworthy software. TOGAF [13] is a comprehensive framework for developing enterprise architectures (e.g., guidelines, patterns, and techniques) based on stakeholder requirements.

Some approaches have been standardized and explicitly focus on certain software quality attributes, mostly considering security. ISO 27001:2013 [11] considers certification based on the development and operation of Information Security Management Systems, and explicitly addresses requirements for secure software development. Common Criteria (ISO 15408) [9] aims at evaluating and certifying software systems with regard to security properties, whereas SSE-CMM (ISO 21827) [10] proposes a maturity model for developing secure software, mainly covering organizational and process aspects. The Building Security In Maturity Model (BSIMM) [2,3] initiative also aims at assessing maturity and describing related activities. Process-independent best practices for developing secure software are proposed in [14,16,18]. Furthermore, some projects, such as OWASP [22] or SHIELDS [17,27], provide methods and tools for detecting, assessing and mitigating security hazards and risks.

To best of our knowledge, existing development methodologies for trustworthy systems typically focus on robustness, correctness and security functionality, while there is a need for a broader view of trustworthiness, taking for instance social and economic aspects into account. Hence, there is potential to enhance and tailor existing development methodologies so that certain aspects of a holistic view on trustworthiness are taken into account.

The Trusted Software Methodology (TSM) [1,4] is the only comprehensive approach that describes processes and guidance for engineering and assessing trustworthy software. It covers multiple quality attributes, and focuses on processes instead of evaluating development artifacts. TSM provides a set of Trust Principles, which describe established development practices or process characteristics that enhance software trustworthiness. A development process can be assessed by means of five different levels of trustworthiness, according to the conformance to the trust principles. Though the principles constitute general best practices, however, the methodology is assumed to be applied following a military standard for software development [4]. In contrast, our focus is on enhancing a broad spectrum of general software development methodologies in order to incorporate the consideration of trustworthiness and to evaluate the practiced process targeting trustworthiness. Yang et al. [33] developed a metamodel that includes trustworthy products dependent on a trustworthy process. But their aim is to provide mechanisms to evaluate the trustworthiness of produced artifact.

An exhaustive overview of development methodologies can be found in [12]. Though Jayaswal and Patton do not specify how these methodologies contribute to the trustworthiness of the product. It documents their generic characteristics and an overview of the historical evolution of different development strategies and life-cycle models.

3 Constrained and Controlled Development Processes

In order to narrow the scope of discussion, we introduced general categories of trustworthy software development. Based on the distinction of introduced process categories, the well-established development methodologies with respect to their suitability to enable trustworthiness-by-design can be discussed further. We may describe three main categories of development as identified, namely:

Uncontrolled: The applications are developed without any special considerations of trustworthiness. This generic approach is very risky regarding the effort (and costs) required for reconstructing, measuring and documenting the elements of trustworthiness of the development process.

Controlled: Trustworthiness is considered, measured and managed along all phases of the development process. It does not necessarily mean that the developed application is trustworthy (or not) but only that trustworthiness has thoroughly been considered with a specific attention.

Constrained: The application is developed in a special way, possibly with a specific language, to assure that the design principles result in verifiable elements of trustworthiness so that specific trustworthiness properties can be (formally) demonstrated.

Although they may in principle all lead to trustworthy systems in the end, it is more likely that this will be the case using a constrained rather than an uncontrolled methodology. Nevertheless, with an uncontrolled methodology the goal would probably not be to create the worlds most trustworthy system, but something that is trustworthy enough for its purpose. Similarly, it may not be feasible to apply a constrained methodology to all development projects. The point is that in general we need to make informed decisions on which "trustworthiness-by-design" steps we choose and apply them based on the characteristics of the methodology at hand.

A number of standards and other activities that address security in the software development process fall into the controlled methodologies category. Security is, in that sense, primarily a set of quality requirements that need to be specified in the first place, and assured along the completely remaining development and operations activities. As such, addressing trustworthiness within the development life-cycle could very much benefit from the activities that are meant to address security since they in general en-compass practices for the assurance of specific (security) properties. There has been little attention, though, in considering the measurably of security-related properties. Some works, e.g., [21,22], have target process enhancements that target security to build a 'secure' software system, describe their measurably capabilities and identify corresponding innovation potential, specifically towards extending security to trustworthiness.

We may consider two distinct applications designed to fulfil a particular task, one application developed in an ad-hoc manner, not following any kind of development methodology, and another one developed using a carefully studied development process and extensively tested (as in [21]). Trustworthiness metrics should allow comparing both applications and give solid evidence as to which of both is "more trustworthy", disregarding the method used to develop each one respectively. We argue that a user should justifiably distrust the first one much more than he should distrust the second one. This trustworthiness is based on the idea that, although we cannot know how trustworthy each application really is beforehand, we do know that the second one could at least have followed a better development process, which in turn is known to help avoiding vulnerabilities. Thus, we can say that the trustworthiness of applications (taking development methodology itself as evidence) is dependent on the development process and methodology and it can make the user confident to some extent.

We will extend this approach in this paper by not taking a specific development practice into account, but rather concentrate on the metrics of trustworthiness properties as used in the comparative example above so that in principle any development process can be used in a controllable way. Thus, using trustworthiness metrics, we can render an arbitrary development process into a controlled one (whereas, of course, for improving the metric values, additional practices or capability patterns may be employed).

4   From Trustworthiness Qualities to Evidences and Certificates

Assessing a software development process to identify its intrinsic qualities generally is a non-trivial task. An assessment methodology must take into account multiple aspects and factors at the same time, from human interactions to the artefacts produced. Therefore, analysing a software development process requires to answer to two important questions: *(a)* which aspects must be considered and *(b)* with which criteria (e.g., metrics) such aspects must be analysed. Starting from the complexity of the problem, established and recognised software measurement approaches and among them notably GQM [30] propose to address both questions at the same time, in order to produce meaningful analysis. Synthesising roughly, the GQM approach is composed by two processes: a top-down refinement of Goals into Questions and then into Metrics, and a bottom-up interpretation of the collected data. The definition of metrics is particularly important: choosing scientifically sound and acknowledged metrics permits to obtain results that are easier to understand and compare with other similar initiatives. In particular, when these conditions are met, the results of the measurement process become objective elements whose interpretation in the bottom-up phase of GQM may lead to meaningful interpretations. Moreover, such objective elements demonstrate the soundness of claims made on the qualities of a software process; when this happens, these elements become *evidences* i.e., elements able to provide assurance about a specific quality. This concept is used in certification, where it is the cornerstone for supporting certificate claims.

Trustworthiness Metrics for Controlled Software Development. Software metrics have a long tradition in software quality, first practical applications date back to the 1980s (e.g. [8]). There are basically two approaches dealing with metrics: *bottom-up* (use what you can measure) and *top-down* (try to measure what you think is valuable). One probably can say that the more mature a software development area is, the better the two converge. With respect to security and trust, unfortunately, there are a number of bottom-up metrics, that often do not match corresponding bottom-down approaches. A typical example is the area of hacker-proofness: whereas one would like to measure observations that express the security against hacks, most available bottom-up metrics give information about attack vectors, attack surfaces, successful attacks etc.

Therefore we decided to follow a top-down approach as proposed by [30] with the GQM methodology to develop metrics. Since subsequently we want to meaningfully aggregate metric values, a number of additional requirements are necessary.

First of all, we assume that all values will be percentage numbers, or alternatively numbers between 0 and 1, similarly to probabilities or assurance factors. The higher the number, the more the aspect/attribute in question should contribute tot he trustworthiness. This way, we will be able to compare values and to perform a number of useful computations. This is a design principle for all top-down metrics, but also needs to apply for all bottom-up metrics that may be considered later on. If we want to use different qualitative levels like "low", "medium" and "high", then there must be a mapping of the qualitative levels to percentage values (reference value = 100, real value = 0, 25, 50, 75 or 100 say for a 4-level qualitative metric (which we think should be avoided as far as possible).

The aggregation of metrics to attribute values is done by computing a weighted sum of the metrics that are considered to belong the attribute. The weight may be interpreted as an importance of the aspect measured in view of the trustworthiness attribute in question, for example when measuring the percentage of function calls that are protected by authorization checks, how much this measurement should be considered to contribute to the "security" attribute.

We have developed significant number of metrics (more than 100 available in a online tool[2]), that may serve as a basis for future use in the context of the controlled software development approach. The online tool on the metrics discusses how they could be used programmatically as well as for a theoretical discussion [20].

Evidences and Assertions. An *Evidence* can be expressed as a proof of a claim that a specific quality can be associated to an *Asset* (i.e. a software or one of its parts). For instance, evidences can be derived from the calculation of specific metrics like software metrics computable on a software artefact (e.g. lines of code, McCabes cyclomatic complexity or others [7]), process or behavioural metrics. However, this definition can also comprise evidences coming from existing certification schemes: in Common Criteria, for example, evidences that evaluators gather are defined as "anything" that can prove the compliance with a mandatory CC requirement or the respect of a criterion: they generally consist of documents, interviews as well as statements made by evaluators on their assessment.

---

[2] http://optet.atc.gr/metrictoolwiki/en/StartingPoints

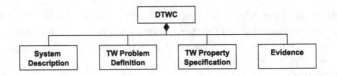

Fig. 1. A schematic representation of DTWC main components

Digital Trustworthiness Certificates. Certificates are means to cater assurance to third-parties that trust the certification body. However, certificates are not always descriptive [31], i.e., they not disclose full information about collected evidences and their collection process. The Digital Trustworthiness Certificate concept (DTWC) [6] permits to describe precisely evidences and their interpretation to support claims on trustworthiness qualities of a software. Such evidences may be product or process metrics, anyway compliant with the definition previously proposed.

The DTWC is a digital artefact that is machine-readable and -understandable, in contrast with traditional certificates that are documents often written in legal terms. It aims at representing claims on the trustworthiness qualities of a software, where trustworthiness is defined as "the objective performance evaluation of the relevant set of quality attributes, based on the evidence from observed system behaviour" [23]. It is based on a Linked Data vocabulary and it is composed by four main parts: system description, trustworthiness problem definition, trustworthiness property specification and evidences (Fig. 1). The system description is scalable in granularity (from methods, libraries and modules up to the whole architecture) and allows for including references to other DTWCs in order to depict exhaustively a software system; the problem definition captures the threats for software qualities that have been considering for a software during its design, development process and runtime execution, similarly to what ISO 27000 proposes for threat modelling. The property specification expresses claims about the qualities of the software (or its specific parts), while the evidence section supports such claims with objective elements. The DTWC is descriptive as it permits a full disclosure of the elements of confidence for a software product or its development process. More details on DTWC can be found at [6]. It is possible, therefore, to create a conceptual link among the qualities that are observable in controlled development methodologies and the possibility to represent them in details through descriptive certificates and in particular through DTWC. Metrics identification and measures are captured as DTWC evidences, that have an explicit link to claims on software/process qualities (the trustworthiness properties) associated to a software or its parts (assets).

5   Use Cases for Lightweight Certificate Based on Trustworthiness Metrics

It is possible to use DTWC, exploiting their machine-intelligibility, in different use cases: be them automatic or human-oriented. For the former case, one can think to DTWC as meta-data providers in software/service discovery or for Linked Data operations. The latter case requires to present DTWC content in a manner that is: *(i)* easily recognizable (ideally visually), *(ii)* simple enough to address properties or objectives that can be grasped intuitively, *(iii)* allows a drill down to look up detailed information that specifies that the certificate actually means in detail and *(iv)* that is used in an intelligent way to support users in selecting applications based on their requirements.

The characteristics of DTWC, as seen in Sect. 4, permits fulfiling all the mentioned requirements. The hierarchical structure of DTWC and its system description permits to describe a software system and its components, their claims and evidences at different granularities, so that for example different software can be analysed selecting a comparable and objective basis. It also permits a hierarchical visualization of the certificate with "zoom-in" to lower levels of detail about the evidences.

The "zoom-in" functionality is helping in the following manner: users can easily perceive the trustworthiness property or objective that is "guaranteed" by the certificate, and optionally, e.g. for experts, to dive into the more detailed description levels. Manufacturers can target one specific, or, if necessary, a set of attributes and/or objectives to get certified. Developers can stay with their own development model, they may need to provide some transparency on their practices to improve measurement results over time if demanded by the market. Finally, regulators can observe the market evolution, and mandate specific properties if considered necessary, without changing the technical means.

A key success factor is the technical separation of the visualization of the certificate on one side, and of the information complexity that is contained in a certificate. Must be different levels of information related to the certified property/objective in question. We currently envisage three levels of information: *(i)* a visual component that can be displayed using graphical means (like the "TV sticker"), *(ii)* a high level descriptive format that uses the metric(s) in question, showing the names and values of the metric and *(iii)* a low level descriptive format, that explains the computation, meaning and possible interpretations of the metric in view of the property/properties in question. This information is *NOT* specific to a software component, and could be retrieved via URI(s) from e.g., the metrics online service.

6   Conclusion and Future Work

In This paper, a new way of demonstrating trustworthiness of software and Internet-based services is described based on individual evidences, either quantitatively using trustworthiness metrics or other types of qualitative evidences. We have applied this research in limited use cases and we can demonstrate their usefulness. The major work that still needs to be done is to perform feasibility studies by applying trustworthiness metrics to larger real life examples and correspondingly improving the metrics over time.

Furthermore, an evaluation and certification process shall be developed to actually implement the independent validation of the certificates. To support an open market development, that process shall be as open as possible. Therefore, the concept of the certification process should allow different approaches in the following dimensions:

- Using different certification authorities (these being, in the language of certification processes according to ISO 17021, the certification bodies, as well as the owners of the technical "CA" in PKI terms), allowing from self-signed certificates, industrial certification bodies up to nation-level certification authorities/bodies if deemed necessary.
- Using different evaluation laboratories, that perform the actual assessment / verification of the metrics values, allowing from the manufacturers' own quality assurance department, industrially driven standards organizations up to specialized accredited evaluation labs.
- Using different scopes and context conditions, as well as choice of metrics (and so evidences), allowing to adapt to different business and maybe also consumer scenarios, in different verticals with different success factors and requirements for trustworthy software or services.

One important question that needs to be specified in a first application of this scenario is the reliability of the overall process. In a first implementation, we would recommend to stick to ISO 17021 and to apply software quality measurement techniques as described in ISO 25021ff., thereby hoping to benefit from the existing infrastructure for accreditation and certification that has been established and has proven to be successful in the market, e.g. for quality management systems, information security management systems, and even Common Criteria certification schemes.

Some success factors still apply, and therefore the results of this analysis rely on a number of assumptions. Further work is needed to define a common taxonomy (specifically, relating properties, attributes, the high-level content of certificates, the description and interpretation of metrics, and so on). To support the adoption of this approach, there is a need to come up with simple scenarios and implementations of the certification process and even the certificates. Correspondingly, further work is needed to specify templates for certificates for some exemplary scenarios that are easy to grasp (e.g. "hacker-proof" by providing a 100 % metric value on the input validation and output sanitization of all interfaces). It is furthermore important to avoid different interpretations of the different information detail "levels" within a certificate between different stakeholders and/or verticals or more generically groups. Therefore, in contrast to the flexibility of the model in terms of objectives measured, or certification reliability, the different "levels of taxonomy" (we currently suggest three levels, as described above) must be fixed from the start.

Acknowledgements. This work is supported by the EU-funded project OPTET (grant no. 317631).

References

1. Amoroso, E., Taylor, C., Watson, J., Weiss, J.: A process-oriented methodology for assessing and improving software trustworthiness. In Proceedings of the 2nd ACM Conference on Computer and Communications Security, CCS 1994, pp. 39–50. ACM, New York (1994)
2. BSIMM-V. The Building Security In Maturity Model. http://www.bsimm.com/
3. Chess, B., Arkin, B.: Software security in practice. IEEE Secur. Priv. 9(2), 89–92 (2011)
4. G. Chisholm, J. Gannon, R. Kemmerer, and J. McHugh. Peer review of the trusted software methodology. Technical report, Argonne National Laboratory, IL, USA, February 1994
5. Di Cerbo, F., Bezzi, M., Kaluvuri, S.P., Sabetta, A., Trabelsi, S., Lotz, V.: Towards a trustworthy service marketplace for the future internet. In: Álvarez, F., Cleary, F., Daras, P., Domingue, J., Galis, A., Garcia, A., Gavras, A., Karnourskos, S., Krco, S., Li, M.-S., Lotz, V., Müller, H., Salvadori, E., Sassen, A.-M., Schaffers, H., Stiller, B., Tselentis, G., Turkama, P., Zahariadis, T. (eds.) FIA 2012. LNCS, vol. 7281, pp. 105–116. Springer, Heidelberg (2012)
6. Di Cerbo, F., Kaluvuri, S.P., Motte, F., Nasser, B., Chen, W., Short, S.: Towards a linked data vocabulary for the certification of software properties. In: 2014 International Conference on Signal-Image Technology & Internet-Based Systems (SITIS), pp. 721–727. IEEE (2014)
7. Fenton, N.E., Pfleeger, S.L.: Software Metrics: A Rigorous and Practical Approach. PWS Publishing Co., Boston (1998)
8. Grady, R.B., Caswell, D.L.: Software Metrics: Establishing a Company-Wide Program. Prentice Hall, Upper Saddle River (1987)
9. International Organization for Standardization. ISO/IEC 15408–1:2009 - Information technology - Security techniques - Evaluation criteria for IT security - Part 1: Introduction and general model (SSE-CMM). http://www.iso.org
10. International Organization for Standardization. ISO/IEC 21827 - Information technology - Security techniques - Systems Security Engineering - Capability Maturity Model (SSE-CMM). http://www.iso.org
11. International Organization for Standardization. Iso/iec 27001:2013- information technology - security techniques - information security management systems - requirements. http://www.iso.org
12. Jayaswal, B.K., Patton, P.C.: Design for Trustworthy Software: Tools, Techniques, and Methodology of Developing Robust Software. Pearson Education, Upper Saddle River (2006)
13. Josey, A.: TOGAF Version 9.1 Enterprise Edition. An Introduction. Technical report, The Open Group (2011)
14. Lipner, S.: The trustworthy computing security development lifecycle. In Proceedings of the 20th Annual Computer Security Applications Conference, ACSAC 2004, pp. 2–13. IEEE Computer Society, Washington (2004)
15. Lotz, V., Kaluvuri, S.P., Di Cerbo, F., Sabetta, A.: Towards security certification schemas for the internet of services. In: 2012 5th International Conference on New Technologies, Mobility and Security (NTMS), pp. 1–5. IEEE (2012)
16. McGraw, G.: Software Security: Building Security In. Addison-Wesley Professional, New York (2006)
17. Meland, P., Ardi, S., Jensen, J., Rios, E., Sanchez, T., Shahmehri, N., Tondel, I.: An architectural foundation for security model sharing and reuse. In: International Conference on Availability, Reliability and Security, 2009, ARES 2009, pp. 823–828, March 2009

18. Microsoft. Security Development Lifecycle. http://www.microsoft.com/security/sdl/default.aspx
19. Mohammadi, N.G., Bandyszak, T., Paulus, S., Meland, P.H., Weyer, T., Pohl, K.: Extending development methodologies with trustworthiness-by-design for socio-technical systems. In: Holz, T., Ioannidis, S. (eds.) Trust 2014. LNCS, vol. 8564, pp. 206–207. Springer, Heidelberg (2014)
20. Mohammadi, N.G., Paulus, S., Bishr, M., Metzger, A., Könnecke, H., Hartenstein, S., Weyer, T., Pohl, K.: Trustworthiness attributes and metrics for engineering trusted internet-based software systems. In: Helfert, M., Desprez, F., Ferguson, D., Leymann, F. (eds.) CLOSER 2013. CCIS, vol. 453, pp. 19–35. Springer, Heidelberg (2014)
21. Neto, A.A., Vieira, M.: Untrustworthiness: a trust-based security metric. In: 2009 Fourth International Conference on Risks and Security of Internet and Systems (CRiSIS), pp. 123–126. IEEE (2009)
22. Open Web Application Security Project (OWASP). CLASP Project (Comprehensive, Light-weight Application Security Process). https://www.owasp.org/index.php/Category:OWASP_CLASP_Project
23. OPTET Consortium. Initial concepts and abstractions to model trustworthiness. Project Deliverable D3.1, OPTET Consortium (2013). http://www.optet.eu
24. Paulus, S., Mohammadi, N.G., Weyer, T.: Trustworthy software development. In: De Decker, B., Dittmann, J., Kraetzer, C., Vielhauer, C. (eds.) CMS 2013. LNCS, vol. 8099, pp. 233–247. Springer, Heidelberg (2013)
25. Potter, B.: Microsoft SDL threat modelling tool. Netw. Secur. **2009**(1), 15–18 (2009)
26. Schmidt, D.: Guest editor's introduction: model-driven engineering. Computer **39**(2), 25–31 (2006)
27. SHIELDS. Detecting known security vulnerabilities from within design and development tools. http://www.shields-project.eu/
28. Sommerville, I.: Software Engineering, 9th edn. Addison-Wesley, Harlow (2010)
29. Sutcliffe, A.: Convergence or competition between software engineering and human computer interaction. In: Seffah, A., Gulliksen, J., Desmarais, M. (eds.) Human-Centered Software Engineering Integrating Usability in the Software Development Lifecycle. HCIS, vol. 8, pp. 71–84. Springer, Netherlands (2005)
30. Van Solingen, R., Basili, V., Caldiera, G., Rombach, H.D.: Goal Question Metric (GQM) Approach. In: Encyclopedia of Software Engineering, John Wiley & Sons, Inc. (2002). doi:10.1002/0471028959.sof142
31. Wallnau, K.: Software component certification: 10 useful distinctions. Technical note. Carnegie Mellon University, Software Engineering Institute (2004)
32. Weigert, T.: Practical experiences in using model-driven engineering to develop trustworthy computing systems. In: IEEE International Conference on Sensor Networks, Ubiquitous, and Trustworthy Computing (SUTC 2006), 5–7 June 2006, pp. 208–217, Taichung, Taiwan (2006)
33. Yang, Y., Wang, Q., Li, M.: Process trustworthiness as a capability indicator for measuring and improving software trustworthiness. In: Wang, Q., Garousi, V., Madachy, R., Pfahl, D. (eds.) ICSP 2009. LNCS, vol. 5543, pp. 389–401. Springer, Heidelberg (2009)

Security and Business Situational Awareness

Roland Rieke[1,2]([✉]), Maria Zhdanova[1], and Jürgen Repp[1]

[1] Fraunhofer Institute SIT, Darmstadt, Germany
{roland.rieke,maria.zhdanova,juergen.repp}@sit.fraunhofer.de
[2] Philipps-Universität Marburg, Marburg, Germany

Abstract. "Security needs to be aligned with business". Business situational awareness is the ability to continually monitor ongoing actions and events related to business operations and estimate the immediate and close-future impact of the new information. This ability is crucial for business continuity and should encompass all associated aspects. Considering the growing dependability of businesses on IT on the one hand, and ever increasing threats on the other, IT security aspects should get adequate attention in the awareness system. We present an approach to raise business situational awareness using an advanced method of predictive security analysis at runtime. It continually observes a system's event stream to find deviations from specified behavior and violations of security compliance rules. Operational models of the key processes are utilized to predict critical security states, evaluate possible countermeasures, and trigger corrective actions. A security information model maintains the security strategy and explains possible deviations from the originating goal. The approach is demonstrated on an industrial scenario from a European research project.

Keywords: Predictive security analysis · Process behavior analysis · Security modeling and simulation · Security monitoring · Security strategy · Security information and event management · Governance and compliance

1 Introduction

Business processes are the most important asset of enterprises, since they provide the basis of the value chain and, thus, define the underlying business model. The Internet today provides an ecosystem, where frequent changes to *business process* models have to be applied, to address changing business needs [31]. This evolving environment, however, also enables new threats and scales up the risks of financial and also physical impact. Thus, business processes must not only be secure, they must be demonstrably so. Situational Awareness (SA) can be viewed as three increasing levels: perception of the elements in the environment, comprehension of the current situation, and projection of future status, that altogether form the basis for decision making [7]. The perception level gives necessary information on the environment recognizing the status and behavior of

© Springer International Publishing Switzerland 2015
F. Cleary and M. Felici (Eds.): CSP Forum 2015, CCIS 530, pp. 103–115, 2015.
DOI: 10.1007/978-3-319-25360-2_9

relevant objects. The comprehension level analyzes and interprets the perceived information in order to identify critical objects and events and determine the current state. The projection level predicts a (close-) future state based on the obtained knowledge to adequately respond to potential problems. All three levels of SA depend on decision maker's goals and context.

In this paper we introduce a flexible and comprehensive modeling approach for business SA that allows us to align business systems with supporting IT and to encompass IT security aspects. This work mainly builds on the Security Strategy Meta Model (SSMM) [24,28] and the Predictive Security Analysis at Runtime (PSA@R) approach [6,23,25], and uses the notion of Enterprise Architecture (EA) as a structured enterprise modeling approach [18]. The SSMM spans all stages of the security monitoring and decision support process, namely: (i) detecting threatening events; (ii) putting them into context of the system state; (iii) explaining their potential impact with respect to the security compliance model; (iv) taking appropriate actions. More specifically, we aim to show that utilizing a model of the prescribed process behavior and the respective compliance rules supports an intelligent security management life-cycle over the whole value creation cycle. The process owners can: (1) assess the achievement of the process objectives better, (2) determine and predict deviations from the planned (prescribed) behavior, (3) monitor and audit the executing process regarding the security policies, (4) assess the treatment of incidents better, (5) identify weak points in the process flow and so better plan corrections of the process flow.

Our Contributions: We extended the SSMM with the asset dimension to align the architecture of the managed system and the security directives related to the critical assets. We describe an implementation of security strategy management based on the SSMM using Security Strategy Processing Component (SSPCs) provided by a prototypical implementation of PSA@R. Moreover, we present new results from the application of PSA@R implemented in the Predictive Security Analyzer (PSA) tool to industrial scenarios. These results demonstrate the integration of security status information into the PSA@R security directives and the co-action of Complex Event Processing (CEP) and PSA for attack detection.

This paper is structured as follows: Sect. 2 explains the background and Sect. 3 presents our systemic approach for business SA and the extended SSMM. Section 4 describes the architecture and functionality of the PSA providing its implementation. Section 5 describes the adaptation of the PSA to industrial scenarios, followed by concluding remarks in Sect. 6.

2   Background

An EA meta model describes the organization of an enterprise encompassing multiple views (structural layers), equally focused on business-related elements, such as business goals and processes, and on application systems and IT infrastructure [18]. A variety of EA frameworks were established in practice and research [13]. From the most cited ones, the Zachman Framework [30], The Open Group Architectural Framework (TOGAF) [32], and Sherwood Applied

Business Security Architecture (SABSA) [29] were evaluated for security engineering. While operational risk management is an important aspect of EA, IT security – being one of the most critical operational risks faced by IT-enabled enterprises – is not considered by the majority of EA frameworks [34]. Thus, though EA helps to reveal sensitive assets and identify (multi-level) dependencies between them, this information needs to be enriched with security concepts.

Modeling concepts for combined views of business, application, physical, and technical information are given in [10], while [27] introduces the use of event-triggered rules for sensing and responding to business situations. A formalized approach to security risk modeling for electronic business processes in [33] comprises simulation aspects, but not the utilization of runtime models. A classification of approaches in the field of Business Process Management (BPM) is given in [1]. According to this classification, the work presented here supports the "check conformance using event data" approach, where information from the process model and the event data is used to identify deviations of runtime behavior from expected behavior. The work on runtime compliance verification for business processes in [15] is complementary to the work presented here.

3   Systemic Approach for Business Situational Security Awareness

A systemic approach for business SA consists of three interrelated parts (see Fig. 1): a *business context* part defined by an EA meta model, a *security information* part given by the Security Information Meta Model (SIMM), and an *operational aspects* part expressed with the SSMM. These models are linked together through model artifacts.

In order to provide a flexible and comprehensive concept for business SA that considers security aspects we adopt a modeling approach introduced in [24,28]. This approach enables a multi-level and cross-domain analysis of security issues and builds upon two interlinked semantic concepts: the SIMM and the SSMM. The SIMM [24] defines a top-down security design process consisting in consecutive definition of four interrelated model parts: (i) high-level (security) goals, (ii) security requirements, (iii) measurement requirements, and (iv) objects of measurement. The SIMM can be viewed as a hierarchy, each level of which refines concepts of higher levels depending on the associated environment. A similar approach - but with a different focus - has been proposed by the project PoSecCo, where a traceable chain of connected policies bridges three different abstraction levels: business policies, IT security policies, and security configurations [2]. In order to obtain system security requirements that convey targeted security goals one would need to employ some procedure for security requirement elicitation [8,17]. Measurement requirements specify how security status of the system, i.e., conformance to given security requirements can be verified (measured). Note that the measurement requirements part of the SIMM is a new structure extending the definition of the Information Security Measurement Model (ISMM) given in the ISO/IEC 27004 standard [11], which is introduced to link the information need to a relevant object of measurement. Operational aspects of the SIMM are covered by the SSMM [28].

The SSMM provides a way for users to define at an abstract level detection rules for security incidents that can be automatically compiled into tool-specific rules, e.g., event correlation rules of a CEP engine. The SSMM has four parts, namely : *on*, : *if*, : *do*, and : *why*, which are derived from the measurement requirements on one hand, and which refer back to the SIMM on the other hand (cf. Fig. 1). The : *on* part specifies *event stream property* or event patterns that indicate a security incident. This part describes anomalies and misuse signatures using parameters extracted from an event stream (channel) together with detection criteria evaluating extracted parameters. The event stream property can be used to express both horizontal event correlation, as steps in a work-flow, and vertical correlation across multiple abstraction levels, e.g., correlation of alerts received from an intrusion detection system with violated security requirement. The : *if* part of the model provides *context information* specifying system state conditions to be validated whenever a (malicious) event pattern is matched. Context information increases the probability to discover targeted attacks and is essential for stateful incident detection, such as practiced in process security analysis. Moreover, the SSMM supports the whole cycle of security incident management including incident response. Its : *do* part models executable *response actions* to be performed when an incident is detected, ranging from notification to autonomous re-configuration of the IT system, e.g., blocking a malicious IP address on a firewall. In order to close the traditional *plan-do-check/study-act* cycle [5], incident detection needs to be linked to the high-level security requirement. This is achieved by the : *why* part of the SSMM, represented by the dotted arrow in Fig. 1. It defines *security pertinence* of an incident and should contain a reference to security concepts specified by the SIMM. The : *why* part helps to estimate the impact of the incident and explains why certain countermeasures are taken. A concrete instance of the SSMM is called Security Strategy Model (SSM) and is made of specific rules, Security Directive (SDs).

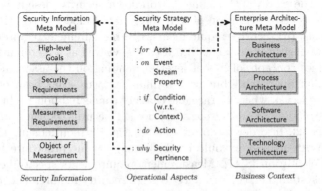

Fig. 1. Modeling approach for business situational awareness

In order to connect the enterprise assets represented by an EA model and the security strategy, we extend the SSMM structure with the : *for* part that provides an explicit *asset reference*. It enables propagation of security requirements as well as systematic tracing of security incidents through the abstraction layers of EA and evaluation of their impact in regard to business goals and processes. This extension can also facilitate operational aspects of creation and management of SDs in the following ways. First, the : *for* part enables easy identification of dependent SDs. Then, an activation of one of the dependent SDs can cause a cascade triggering of others even if it is not explicitly defined in the : *do* part. The latter means that an incident can be detected even if some sensors implementing the : *on* part in dependent SDs are compromised. Moreover, the link between EA and the SSMM allows completeness analysis of SDs in order to reveal missing or redundant SDs and ensure that all critical security properties are covered. It also aids in detection of conflicting response actions which can block operations within the enterprise if realized. Finally, an explicit asset reference in an SD helps to identify optimal measurement points, including domain-specific sensors and physical sensors, ormulate context conditions related only to a particular asset and to update is information if the underlying EA changes, e.g. new sensors appear or security systems are deployed. Thus, the extension to the SSMM allows an enterprise to increase overall SA and to respond to security incidents in a more robust and adequate way due to closer semantic relations and mutual information exchange between security concepts and enterprise structures. In the following we use the term SSMM to refer to the extended SSMM.

4   Security Strategy Processing

Conceptually, the implementation of SSMM processing is composed of SSPCs [24]. One specific component called PSA [6,23,25] has been developed by the authors of this paper. At runtime, the PSA *observes* the operation of a managed system by analyzing events received from this system. A novel capability in this approach is that it utilizes an operational process specification to compute the pre-planned process behavior depending on the actual state of an observed system. Deviations from the expected behavior trigger *uncertainty management* and possibly alerts. Formally, the behavior of the operational process model is described by a Reachability Graph (RG) [19], also referred to as Labelled Transition System (LTS) [20]. PSA@R uses the RG to *predict the close-future behavior of the process instance*. A subgraph of the RG starting with the current state of the process instance can always be computed on-the-fly based on the formal process model. The *prediction depth* is the depth of this subgraph starting from the current state.

The PSA supports the specification and on-the-fly check of security compliance rules as well as visualization of the current security status. Possible close-future process actions can be predicted based on the operational process specification and the current process state as reflected in the model. This knowledge about the expected behavior is used to predict upcoming critical states regarding given security compliance rules. This *judgment* whether the observed system behaves according to the given rules enables proactive reactions for risk mitigation. Figure 2 shows the architecture of the PSA and its interaction with the observed system as well as other systems in the environment that can play the role of SSPCs. The *PSA modeler* provides the user interface for model management and visualization of the current system state, and the *PSA core* performs process security analysis at runtime. For the applications presented in this paper, the PSA was deployed in the next-generation Security Information Event Management (SIEM) architecture MASSIF [35] to perform (high-level) security event processing and anomaly detection on the business application (service) layer.

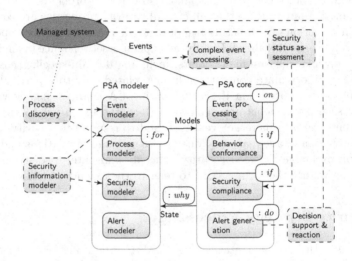

Fig. 2. Architecture and environment of the predictive security analyzer

The *event processing component* of the PSA core processes the : *on* part of the SSMM. It maps the events to the corresponding process instance, and creates abstract events containing only information that is relevant for security processing. This component can optionally be supported by external CEP. In the MASSIF framework, the coaction of CEP and PSA for attack patterns detection was realized by two components, namely Generic Event Translation (GET) [4] for distributed collection and preliminary correlation of raw events and a high-performance CEP [3] for correlation. The PSA *behavior conformance component* and the *security compliance component* process the : *if* part of the SSMM. The abstract events are used by the *behavior conformance component* to update the respective state of process instance models reflecting the actual state of the running processes and behavior anomalies are identified. By executing the security model the *security compliance component* identifies process states critical from the security perspective. The security compliance component can optionally be supported by external components for *security status assessment*.

In MASSIF this was realized by the Attack Modelling and Security Evaluation Component (AMSEC) [12]. If a process anomaly or a security critical state is detected or predicted, the PSA *alert generation component*, which implements the : *do* part of the SSMM, triggers a security event using the mapping configured in the alert model. In MASSIF, these alerts were forwarded to the Decision Support and Reaction (DSR) component [9] for countermeasure selection and response. Backward references within the process and security models allow to visualize the current process state with the PSA *process modeler component* which is related to the : *for* part of the SSMM and the security state within the *security modeler component* of the PSA. The PSA modeler manages reference to the originating goal with the help of a project description. This provides basic functionality for the : *why* part of the SSMM.

5   Industrial Setups: Lessons Learned

Based on experiences with application of an early prototype in a logistics scenario [6], we have applied the PSA tool in several use cases, each of which allowed us to examine a particular aspect of PSA@R in a realistic industrial setup [16]. The application scenarios related to four industrial domains: (i) managed enterprise service infrastructures for outsourced IT services [22]; (ii) mobile money transfer services provided by a mobile network operator [26]; (iii) the Olympic Games IT infrastructure management [21]; (iv) critical infrastructure process control (on the example of a storage dam in a hydroelectric power plant) [4]. (Mis)use cases made available for each domain by scenario providers overed one or several steps of the proposed security analysis cycle, rom behavior conformance monitoring to detection of security violations and prediction of security-critical situations in the near future. In the range of the applications presented in this section, the PSA was deployed as a model management component of the next-generation SIEM architecture MASSIF to perform (high-level) security event processing and anomaly detection on the business application (service) layer [35]. Collection and preliminary correlation of raw events were carried out by other MASSIF components, such as GET [4] and CEP [3]. Alerts produced by the PSA were forwarded to the DSR system which implemented countermeasure selection and response mechanisms [9]. In this section we exemplarily summarize our experience using an industrial scenario from the MASSIF project.

5.1   Olympic Games

In today's media society, the Olympic Games have become one of the most profitable global media events. Olympics media diffusion, international dimension, and symbolic value constitutes a lucrative target for attackers. As a consequence, security has become a top priority [21]. In the MASSIF project, we have investigated security provisioning for Olympic Games services accessible over the Internet, such as the accreditation and sport entries applications. Considering high security risks, it is reasonable to assume that extensive efforts are made to protect the IT infrastructure of the Olympic Games from both persistent and emerging threats. In particular, we considered a misuse case, which involved a targeted "low-and-slow" (persistent) attack on a web application server providing the accreditation service for participants [14,22]. The adversary is aware that the IT infrastructure is under continuous security monitoring, therefore, she executes multiple low profile actions distributed over longer period of time. In our trial setup, the adversary first compromises a sports entries web server in order to brute-force a local administrative account. When this attempt fails, she performs port scanning to discover an open LDAP port on a back-end authentication server. The adversary launches a command injection attack to obtain root access on the authentication server. She retrieves a list of user credentials and resorts to exhaustive search on the accreditation web server to find some user account with sufficient privileges for the accreditation application.

Assets (: *for*). The accreditation application processing accreditation data is the critical asset targeted. In order to gain access to the accreditation data other entities in the IT infrastructure – the sport entries server and authentication server – get compromised to provide a launch site for the final attack step.

Event Stream (: *on*). Security events were generated using a testbed that reproduced the Olympic Games IT infrastructure with deployed security controls. These events were sent to the CEP component of the MASSIF SIEM where they were correlated over different time intervals to reveal adversarial behavior patterns. If malicious activity was detected, the CEP produced an alarm with a specific identifier (e.g., *data_tampering*, *privilege_escalation*) which was forwarded to the PSA for further correlation. The following alarm identifiers referring to particular attack steps were used:

Condition(: *if*). The PSA aggregates alarms generated by different security controls in the observed infrastructure evaluates the security state in regard to the specified "low-and-slow" attack and predicts near future security-critical states and potential security violations by means of the security monitor presented in Fig. 3. The monitor automaton has two critical states – *crashes_edirectory* and *unusual_activity* – in which the PSA generates a security alert.

Action (: *do*). If a critical state of the monitor automaton (see Fig. 3) is reached, the PSA generates a corresponding security alert that was forwarded to the DSR system, which blocked the IP address of the adversary.

Security Pertinence (: *why*). In this case, the goal is to "prevent unauthorized access to the accreditation data".

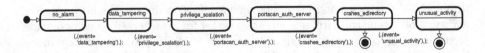

Fig. 3. Security monitor for the Olympic Games scenario

5.2 Lessons Learned

The main problem we faced during the adaptation to the use case scenarios is that none of them a priori involved either process-aware information systems or process specifications. Another problem concerns synchronization and ordering of events coming from different systems with different time bases. Thus, a point of particular interest regarding these industrial setups is exploitation of process-aware security controls similar to the PSA in "process-unaware" environments that can often be seen in the wild. In the Olympic Games scenario, it was not possible to relate the events from different event sources to the respective process instance because the needed event attributes were missing. As in this case, the application provider could not modify the involved systems, the modeled process behavior thus did not reflect the business process but rather an attack process (cf. Fig. 4). The scenario provider reported that once the models are completed, the regular use is fairly simple [16].

Fig. 4. Reachability graph of the attack process in the Olympic Games scenario

A general finding of our work on runtime security assessment is that the traditional *plan-do-check/study-act* cycle [5] needs to be extended, when applied to information security measurement. In the *plan* phase, it should not only establish the objectives, identify security requirements, and analyse the design of the system, but also *plan runtime measurements*. In the *do* phase, it should not only analyse the configuration of he implemented plan, and verify that the goals are met, but also *provide data for runtime analysis*. In the *check/study* phase, it should *identify and study deviations f measured from expected results, check for compliance*, and *forecast critical behavior*. Finally, in the *act* phase, it should analyse security consequences, etermine their root causes, and trigger corrective actions.

6 Conclusion and Research Directions

We have argued that business goals and compliance requirements, which create obligations for security management, need a meta model - such as SSMM - that consolidates the necessary security strategy information. Therefore, we extended the SSMM, which has been introduced in [24,28], with an EA model to link the architecture of the managed system and the security directives defined for the critical assets. We have exemplarily shown, how to implement the systemic approach for security strategy management based on the SSMM, by means of a mapping of components of our PSA prototype to SSPCs.

The PSA provides early awareness about deviations of a running process from expected behavior - as specified by the model - and generates triggers for decision support and reaction. As security relies on the compliance of actual behavior with the given specifications, this early detection of changes and reaction elevates security of the process in question. In combination with other novel applications, the PSA enables anticipatory impact analysis, decision support, and impact mitigation by adaptive configuration of countermeasures.

In particular, we have demonstrated on an industrial scenario, how the SSMM can be used in a framework of SSPCs, to observe system and process behavior, detect anomalies, and provide situational awareness not only on an infrastructure but also up to business process level. This scenario also demonstrates the co-action of CEP and PSA and the integration of security status information into PSA security monitoring for attack process detection. The external security status information from AMSEC enriches the context awareness. It is used by the PSA to improve the assessment of the security status of the observed process and thus facilitates the prediction of security policy violations in close future.

Results published in [23] confirm that model-based analysis as implemented in the PSA prototype is applicable and fast enough for security analysis of important real-world applications at runtime. However, in order to apply our PSA@R method easily, systems, applications, and processes should be *designed for security assessment at runtime*. The approach has been validated specifically with respect to security concerns but is also applicable to on-the-fly analysis of generic compliance and dependability requirements. Further results published in [36], where we compared PSA@R with classical fraud detection approaches, indicate that we can achieve better recognition performance.

For future work, we plan to investigate the adaptability of our security strategy management approach to decentralized Internet of things ecosystems, where traditional centralized security management concepts will not be applicable and - from the privacy perspective - not even desirable.

Acknowledgments. This research was supported by the European Commission in the context of the project MASSIF (ID 257475) and the German Federal Ministry of Education and Research in the project ACCEPT (ID 01BY1206D).

References

1. van der Aalst, W.M.P.: Business process management: a comprehensive survey. ISRN Softw. Eng. **2013**, 37 (2013)
2. Arsac, W., Laube, A., Plate, H.: Policy chain for securing service oriented architectures. In: Di Pietro, R., Herranz, J., Damiani, E., State, R. (eds.) DPM 2012 and SETOP 2012. LNCS, vol. 7731, pp. 303–317. Springer, Heidelberg (2013)
3. Callau-Zori, M., Jiménez-Peris, R., Gulisano, V., Papatriantafilou, M., Fu, Z., Patiño Martínez, M.: STONE: a Stream-based DDoS defense framework. In: Proceedings of the 28th Annual ACM Symposium on Applied Computing SAC 2013, pp. 807–812. ACM, New York (2013)

4. Coppolino, L., D'Antonio, S., Formicola, V., Romano, L.: Enhancing SIEM technology to protect critical infrastructures. In: Hämmerli, B.M., Kalstad Svendsen, N., Lopez, J. (eds.) CRITIS 2012. LNCS, vol. 7722, pp. 10–21. Springer, Heidelberg (2013)

5. Deming, W.E.: The new economics for industry, government, education / W. Edwards Deming, Massachusetts Institute of Technology, Center for Advanced Engineering Study, Cambridge (1993)

6. Eichler, J., Rieke, R.: Model-based situational security analysis. In: Proceedings of the 6th International Workshop on Models@run.time at the ACM/IEEE 14th International Conference on Model Driven Engineering Languages and Systems (MODELS 2011), CEUR Workshop Proceedings, vol. 794, pp. 25–36. RWTH Aachen (2011)

7. Endsley, M.: Toward a theory of situation awareness in dynamic systems. Hum. Factors 37(1), 32–64 (1995)

8. Fuchs, A., Rieke, R.: Identification of security requirements in systems of systems by functional security analysis. In: Casimiro, A., de Lemos, R., Gacek, C. (eds.) Architecting Dependable Systems VII. LNCS, vol. 6420, pp. 74–96. Springer, Heidelberg (2010)

9. Granadillo, G., Jacob, G., Debar, H., Coppolino, L.: Combination approach to select optimal countermeasures based on the rori index. In: 2012 Second International Conference on Innovative Computing Technology (INTECH), pp. 38–45 (2012)

10. Innerhofer-Oberperfler, F., Breu, R.: Using an enterprise architecture for it risk management. In: Eloff, J.H.P., Labuschagne, L., Eloff, M.M., Venter, H.S. (eds.) ISSA, pp. 1–12. ISSA, Pretoria (2006)

11. Iso Iec: ISO/IEC 27004:2009 - Information technology - Security techniques - Information security management - Measurement (2009)

12. Kotenko, I., Chechulin, A.: Attack modeling and security evaluation in SIEM systems. In: International Transactions on Systems Science and Applications, vol. 8. SIWN Press, December 2012

13. Lange, M., Mendling, J.: An experts' perspective on enterprise architecture goals, framework adoption and benefit assessment. In: 2011 15th IEEE International Enterprise Distributed Object Computing Conference Workshops (EDOCW), pp. 304–313, August 2011

14. Llanes, M., Prieto, E., Diaz, R., Coppolino, L., Sergio, A., Cristaldi, R., Achemlal, M., Gharout, S., Gaber, C., Hutchison, A., Dennie, K.: Scenario requirements (public version). Technical report, FP7-257475 MASSIF European project, April 2011

15. Maggi, F.M., Montali, M., Westergaard, M., van der Aalst, W.M.P.: Monitoring business constraints with linear temporal logic: an approach based on colored automata. In: Rinderle-Ma, S., Toumani, F., Wolf, K. (eds.) BPM 2011. LNCS, vol. 6896, pp. 132–147. Springer, Heidelberg (2011)

16. MASSIF project consortium: Acquisition and evaluation of the results. Deliverable D2.3.3, FP7-257475 MASSIF European project, September 2013

17. Mellado, D., Blanco, C., Sánchez, L.E., Fernández-Medina, E.: A systematic review of security requirements engineering. Comput. Stand. Interfaces 32(4), 153–165 (2010)

18. Nightingale, D.J., Rhodes, D.H.: Enterprise systems architecting: emerging art and science within engineering systems. In: MIT Engineering Systems Symposium, March 2004

19. Ochsenschläger, P., Rieke, R.: Abstraction based verification of a parameterised policy controlled system. In: Gorodetsky, V., Kotenko, I., Skormin, V.A. (eds.) Computer Network Security, Communications in Computer and Information Science, vol. 1, pp. 228–241. Springer, Heidelberg (2007)
20. Peled, D.A.: Software Reliability Methods, 1st edn. Springer, Heidelberg (2001)
21. Prieto, E., Diaz, R., Romano, L., Rieke, R., Achemlal, M.: MASSIF: a promising solution to enhance olympic games IT security. In: Georgiadis, C.K., Jahankhani, H., Pimenidis, E., Bashroush, R., Al-Nemrat, A. (eds.) ICGS3/e-Democracy 2012. LNICST, vol. 99, pp. 139–147. Springer, Heidelberg (2011)
22. Rieke, R., Coppolino, L., Hutchison, A., Prieto, E., Gaber, C.: Security and reliability requirements for advanced security event management. In: Kotenko, I., Skormin, V. (eds.) MMM-ACNS 2012. LNCS, vol. 7531, pp. 171–180. Springer, Heidelberg (2012)
23. Rieke, R., Repp, J., Zhdanova, M., Eichler, J.: Monitoring security compliance of critical processes. In: 2014 22th Euromicro International Conference on Parallel, Distributed and Network-Based Processing (PDP), pp. 525–560. IEEE Computer Society, February 2014
24. Rieke, R., Schütte, J., Hutchison, A.: Architecting a security strategy measurement and management system. In: Proceedings of the Workshop on Model-Driven Security MDsec 2012, pp. 2:1–2:6. ACM, New York (2012)
25. Rieke, R., Stoynova, Z.: Predictive security analysis for event-driven processes. In: Kotenko, I., Skormin, V. (eds.) MMM-ACNS 2010. LNCS, vol. 6258, pp. 321–328. Springer, Heidelberg (2010)
26. Rieke, R., Zhdanova, M., Repp, J., Giot, R., Gaber, C.: Fraud detection in mobile payment utilizing process behavior analysis. In: 2013 Eighth International Conference on Availability, Reliability and Security (ARES), pp. 662–669. IEEE Computer Society (2013)
27. Schiefer, J., Rozsnyai, S., Rauscher, C., Saurer, G.: Event-driven rules for sensing and responding to business situations. In: Jacobsen, H.A., Mühl, G., Jaeger, M.A. (eds.) DEBS. ACM International Conference Proceeding Series, vol. 233, pp. 198–205. ACM (2007)
28. Schütte, J., Rieke, R., Winkelvos, T.: Model-based security event management. In: Kotenko, I., Skormin, V. (eds.) MMM-ACNS 2012. LNCS, vol. 7531, pp. 181–190. Springer, Heidelberg (2012)
29. Sherwood, J., Clark, A., Lynas, D.: Enterprise Security Architecture: A Business-Driven Approach. CMP Books, San Francisco (2005)
30. Sowa, J.F., Zachman, J.A.: Extending and formalizing the framework for information systems architecture. IBM Syst. J. 31(3), 590–616 (1992)
31. Tallon, P.: Inside the adaptive enterprise: an information technology capabilities perspective on business process agility. Inf. Technol. Manag. 9(1), 21–36 (2008)
32. The Open Group: TOGAF Standard Version 9.1 (2012). http://pubs.opengroup.org/architecture/togaf9-doc/arch/. Accessed 24 May 2015
33. Tjoa, S., Jakoubi, S., Goluch, G., Kitzler, G., Goluch, S., Quirchmayr, G.: A formal approach enabling risk-aware business process modeling and simulation. IEEE Trans. Serv. Comput. 4(2), 153–166 (2011)
34. TOGAF-SABSA Integration WG: TOGAF and SABSA Integration. Whitepaper. The Open Group, The SABSA Institute, October 2011

35. Verissimo, P., et al.: Massif architecture document. Technical report, FP7-257475 MASSIF European project, April 2012. http://www.massif-project.eu/sites/default/files/deliverables/MASSIF_Architecturedocument_v15_final.zip. Accessed 24 May 2015

36. Zhdanova, M., Repp, J., Rieke, R., Gaber, C., Hemery, B.: No smurfs: Revealing fraud chains in mobile money transfers. In: Proceedings of 2014 International Conference on Availability, Reliability and Security, ARES 2014, pp. 11–20. IEEE Computer Society (2014)

The Trust Problem in Modern Network Infrastructures

Ludovic Jacquin[1], Antonio Lioy[2(✉)], Diego R. Lopez[3],
Adrian L. Shaw[1], and Tao Su[2]

[1] Hewlett-Packard Laboratories, Bristol, UK
[2] Politecnico di Torino, Torino, Italy
lioy@polito.it
[3] Teléfonica I+D, Madrid, Spain

Abstract. SDN and NFV are modern techniques to implement networking infrastructures and can be used also to implement other advanced functionalities, such as the protection architecture designed by the SECURED project. This paper discusses a couple of techniques – trustworthy network infrastructure monitoring and remote attestation of virtual machines – useful towards a trusted and secure usage of SDN and NFV.

Keywords: SDN · NFV · Remote attestation · Trust · Security

1 Introduction

Network infrastructure is quickly evolving from a hardware-based switch-only layer to a full-fledged computational system able to perform several tasks, switching packets being just one, although a very important one. This evolution is permitted by the advent of two new architectures, namely SDN and NFV.

SDN (Software-Defined Networking) is one particular approach to provide virtualised traffic routing and unified network flow management across hardware and software-based networking components. The principal design of SDN is to virtualise the existing control and data planes by moving the control part away from all network elements to a centralised node in the network, known as the *SDN controller*.

NFV (Network Functions Virtualisation) proposes to virtualise several classes of network node functions into generic building-blocks (to be run as virtual machines on commodity hardware) to be connected for creating various network services. NFV typically exploits SDN to create custom overlay networks connecting the various network functions and in turn SDN can use NFV to host its controllers and applications.

SDN and NFV can be used also for non network-related functions: an example is provided by the SECURED project [1] which uses SDN to create a custom network path for each user to interconnect its network-hosted security controls, that may be executed in a NFV infrastructure. Purpose of this project is to create

F. Cleary and M. Felici (Eds.): CSP Forum 2015, CCIS 530, pp. 116–127, 2015.
DOI: 10.1007/978-3-319-25360-2_10

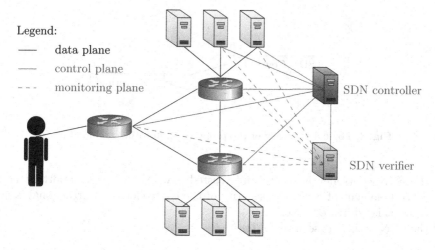

Fig. 1. A typical SDN topology, enhanced with a SDN verifier.

a user-oriented security environment, protecting the user's traffic independent of the specific user device and network access point. As SDN and NFV are critical elements for SECURED, it is investigating techniques to improve their trustworthiness and security and a first analysis and proposal is reported here (Fig. 1).

2 Trustworthy Monitoring Architecture for SDN

The usage of SDN introduces new network abstractions and high-level primitives but this creates a trust gap for administrators as they cannot easily assess the correctness of enforced device configurations. We present here a monitoring architecture for SDN to bridge this semantic gap, with the additional goal to be both trustworthy and automated, such that administrators only need to act upon detection of faulty behaviour. The proposed monitoring architecture introduces an out-of-band *SDN verifier*, from the control plane perspective, to automatically and continuously attest the enforced SDN rules by the network elements.

2.1 Introducing the SDN Verifier

In a typical SDN topology, network elements are both hardware- and software-based, with a hierarchy of controllers to program them all. As we want to address the security and trust concerns of this new layer, we define the following attacker model:

1. an attacker can modify the software stack of a network element;
2. hardware attacks cannot be performed, in particular physical links are deemed secure;

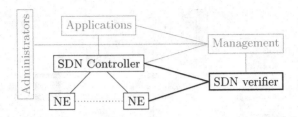

Fig. 2. Logical overview of the proposed monitoring architecture

3. the SDN controller is secure and trusted – whilst it is an important and central element of SDN, the security of the controller is an orthogonal issue to what is addressed here.
4. the SDN verifier is secure and trusted.

The introduction of the SDN verifier requires a new monitoring plane which will be used to exchange attestation data from the network elements. A special part of this monitoring plane is the connection between the verifier and the controller(s): it is used by the verifier to retrieve the expected SDN configuration of the network elements. With regards to the attacker model considered, we keep the same assumption as the controller.

In the control hierarchy, the verifier remains in the same network as the SDN controller and the network elements, as depicted in Fig. 2. We envision that it would report to the management components, which in turn inform the administrator and potentially SDN applications. The application has the logic and knowledge of the network topology, to act on faulty behaviour automatically if needed.

From a functional perspective, the SDN verifier focuses on re-establishing trust in the network elements by attesting their software stack and the SDN configuration they are currently enforcing at the dataplane. Since the main tasks of the controller and network elements are to route the traffic through the dataplane and do performance critical tasks, we choose to alleviate this pressure by offloading the computational complexity to the SDN Verifier. Whilst the verifier–controller interface is quite trivial as most implementation already support that through a web interface, the proposed monitoring architecture needs an embedded monitor inside each network element.

2.2 Network Element Monitoring

The verifier relies on the attestation agent installed in each network element to locally retrieve and package the monitoring data back to the verifier. Since a software-only solution would be prone to a wide range of software attacks, our design uses a trusted device inside the network element. This trusted device is generally immutable and is used as a basis for trust, which is leveraged by the verifier to attest the network element and its behaviour. The trusted device must provide a hardware-based identity and enable the creation of a *Core Root of Trust*

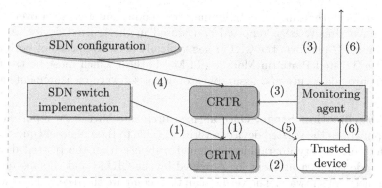

1: Attestation measurements   4: OpenFlow rules inspection
2: Secure storage of measurements 5: Dynamic configuration measurements
3: SDN verifier challenge   6: SDN verifier response

Fig. 3. Network element component architecture target

for Reporting (CRTR), a component which measures the dynamic configurations related to network flow rules that are currently enforced.

Hardware-based Identity. The network element identity is primarily used to derive a pair of public/private keys used to provide integrity and authentication of the monitoring data. For instance, the IEEE 802.1AR already provides examples of facilitating secure device identity provisioning. The identity is provisioned at installation time inside the trusted device with the corresponding derived private key. This identity allows the SDN verifier to check the authenticity of the attestation proof coming from the trusted device and to check the integrity of the measurement reports. The methods of identity distribution and management are not covered as part of this paper.

Measured Boot. One way of assessing the software state of a computer is to measure every trusted piece of software before it is loaded during device start-up. This is known as a *measured boot*. This is achieved by augmenting the boot process of the machine to cryptographically measure executable software at load time and securely report the result to a trusted device prior to transferring execution to the loaded software. The subsequent piece of measured software can in turn load and measure more software. This process is repeated for each piece of software loaded on the platform, creating what is commonly known as a *chain of trust*. Since the trusted device keeps logs of all software executed on the platform, it is able to report all the measurements of the configurations since early in the boot process. Recursively, the measured boot relies on a small combination of hardware and software that must be implicitly trusted to measure software running on the platform. This minimum combination constitutes the *Core Root of Trust for Measurement (CRTM)*. It is fundamental that the CRTM implements a secure storage capability that cannot be tampered with by other software on the platform, such that any potentially malicious code cannot erase or overwrite logs that have already been reported and stored in the trusted device. As an example, on a PC platform the CRTM has typically been composed of both the BIOS and a Trusted Platform Module (TPM), both of which must be trusted in order to provide secure and assurable storage of software measurements and secrets.

Remote Verification Stage. Once all measurements have been reported by each component to the trusted device, a verifier is able to then remotely query the trusted device. The cryptographically signed response from the trusted device should include the measurement log provided by the CRTM and all subsequent measured pieces of software. The verifier can then compare the received logs with well-known measurements corresponding to a measurement database of trusted software components (and states). It is important to note that with a measured boot approach, the verifier must attest each piece of software to verify that nothing previously loaded was unknown or untrusted software. Thus, in order to verify if the operating system is in a trusted state, all the logs of previously executed software must be asserted as known and trusted software.

Attestation Agent. Its main goal is to relay the incoming challenges and outgoing responses between the verifier and the CRTR. It is not a trusted component in the monitoring architecture since the verifier's challenge is used by the trusted device when creating the attestation proof. Any tampering of the challenge or the response would be detected by the SDN verifier.

Core Root of Trust for Reporting (CRTR). The role of the CRTR is to inspect the forwarding table state of the SDN switch implementation in a network element and report it to the SDN verifier. The CRTR is eventually loaded as part of the platform's trusted computing base. Ideally, the CRTR needs to be one-way isolated from the network element implementation. For instance, the CRTR must be able to inspect the VLAN routing tables and system configurations, but the rest of the switch system must not be able to interfere or influence the CRTR functionality, The isolation of the CRTR is either enforced using a hardware mechanism, or attested through a CRTM. The full combination of the CRTR, the agent and the trusted device are illustrated in Fig. 2.

With the addition of the SDN Verifier and the embedded reporting mechanism inside the network elements, a software-defined network can be more strongly attested for (A) correctness of firmware and software at the data plane, and (B) correct enforcement of dynamic configurations, such as VLAN forwarding tables.

2.3 Prototype Implementation

Let us now focus on the trade-offs done during the implementation of a hardware switch prototype and show the equivalent implementation for a virtual SDN switch, such as OvS [2].

For the prototype, we made two major technological choices: (i) we rely on a TPM as the trusted device (and we use the well-known Trusted Computing

Group methods for the CRTM), and (ii) the monitoring agent uses SNMP to communicate with the SDN verifier. Both technologies present the main advantage to be widely deployed world wide. The downside of the TPM is its performance: in our hardware switch prototype, the remote attestation exchange (over SNMP) takes around one second, where most of the latency comes from the digital signature during the TPM Quote operation (which can take as long as 600 ms).

In the meantime, we are evaluating three approaches for a software SDN switch attestation. TPM remains our choice for the trusted device, especially with the existing software environment around it, namely TrustedGRUB [3] and IMA [4]. The main point we are investigating is the CRTR to introspect the "vswitchd" context. We will evaluate three different approaches: (i) full kernel-based integrity monitor, that routinely inspect the memory of the OvS process; (ii) split integrity monitor, that relies on a small kernel module for the memory introspection and moves the processing logic in a user–space agent; (iii) full user–space monitor, if the monitor can access directly the OvS memory space.

3   NFV and Virtual Machine Attestation

Any NFV service deployment requires the onboarding, activation and start-up of a set of virtualised elements that will be run on a uniform infrastructure supporting the virtualised execution environment (the *NFV Infrastructure, NFVI*). Furthermore, these elements have to be connected to other elements according to a given network topology, that will be dynamically created by requesting it to the *Virtual Infrastructure Manager (VIM)*, which typically would create it by means of SDN. In this environment it is obvious the need for applying procedures to verify the integrity of the system (the whole NFV service deployment) by the appropriate attestation of the NFV architectural elements, including software and firmware images and associated supporting security sub-systems that will run to instantiate individual *VNFs (Virtual Network Functions)* and their composition into a NFV service. Since these procedures will have to be executed by the *Management and Orchestration (MANO)* stack in charge of the service deployment they have to support remote attestation mechanisms and, more specifically, they have to apply cryptographic techniques to verify system integrity.

NFV remote attestation requires identifying the root(s) of trust, establishing a chain of trust for the NFVI, the individual VNFs, and the MANO subsystems, and verification of the trust chain, so the MANO stack components can verifiably establish a sufficient level of assurance in the different software elements constituting the VNFs and the service(s) that use them. While exist standards and best practices for attestation in physical environments (TPM, TCG, . . .), a detailed assessment of their applicability is needed due to the extensive use of virtualisation techniques, the scale of VNF composition, and the requirement to perform network topology attestation. The NFV Security Problem Statement [5] describes secure boot and secure crash among key issues for guaranteeing a secure NFV operation, while the NFV Security and Trust Guidance [6] directly mentions attestation mechanisms. Several NFV use cases [7] and reported experiments [8] describe situations in which VNFs are dynamically on-boarded, updated or modified, and a proper verification of their correct provenance is an essential step in these procedures.

The attestation steps may be specific to the level of assurance to be established, which, in turn, depends on the nature of the particular network function, the service it supports, and the different parties involved in its instantiation. Furthermore, different local and remote procedures may apply depending on whether the elements in the supporting infrastructure are trusted. To establish a set of common NFV attestation technologies it will be necessary to address the following aspects:

- define the required levels of assurance;
- identify the assumed capabilities in the NFVI (e.g. TPM, secure boot, ...);
- assign the operational procedures to be applied at each layer of the MANO stack;
- specify how attestation requirements will be expressed in the different NFV descriptors, for the NFVI, individual VNFs, and services;
- specify the information model to exchange attestation requests and data at the reference points in the NFV architecture framework.

Among all these challenges, we currently focus on attestation of virtual machines as it is a fundamental problem for NFV trustworthiness.

3.1   Virtual Machine Attestation

Attestation of physical computing platforms is possible in various ways. A very common one is to exploit the Trusted Platform Module (TPM), a special chip available on most hardware platforms. It is used to provide secure storage, integrity measurement, and reporting. The TPM offers secure storage in the form of *Platform Configuration Registers* (PCRs) that can only be accessed with specific commands. Integrity measurement consists of computing the digest of target files and accumlating the values into the PCRs with a specific command (*extend*).

The action of reporting the integrity of the platform is called *Attestation* and is mostly useful in its *Remote Attestation* form, which is requested by a different network entity that wants evidence about the current software status of the attested platform. The TPM then makes a digital signature over the values of a subset of PCRs to prove to the remote entity the integrity and authenticity of the platform configuration. In this way, the evidence provided to other party is reliable and authentic. It is bound with the hardware TPM, which cannot be forged by others.

Attestation comprises three phases: *measurement, attestation* and *verification*. Previous studies about attesting VMs mainly focus on the first two steps, how to measure the system [4,9], and how to properly attest the results [10,11], but few address the verification problem. Actually, most works do not provide information of how to verify the measurement properly. Binary-based attestation is the most popular solution, which extends the measurements into PCRs residing inside the TPM. Subsequently, verifier compares these PCR binary values with golden ones. This approach can provide high security assurance, but need complex management because the PCR values are order sensitive. Unlike the booting process (where the components are loaded one after another in a specific order), during normal usage the execution of software happens in random order, so PCR values verification could easily fail even though integrity is not compromised.

Attesting VMs is a difficult task as they do not have direct access to the hardware and hence to the TPM, which is the critical component for attestation. Even if direct access to the TPM could be provided, the number of PCRs would be insufficient for the number of VMs normally activated on a single hardware platform.

A first approach to solve this problem is to emulate the whole functionality of a physical TPM by using a custom software module. In this way, this module can be used to attest multiple VMs with just one hardware TPM. This is the *vTPM* [10] approach (Fig. 4) where each VM has a *client side TPM driver*, which VMs send their TPM commands to. A *server side TPM driver* is running in a special VM on top of the hypervisor; this server-side driver collects the data from the client-side driver, and sends them to the vTPM manager. The vTPM manager is in charge of creating vTPM instances and multiplexing requests from VMs to their associated vTPM instances. Since the vTPM instance number is prepended on the server side, a VM cannot forge packets and try to get access to another vTPM instance not associated with itself. This solution has been implemented in XEN [12].

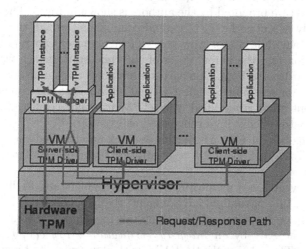

Fig. 4. The vTPM architecture [10].

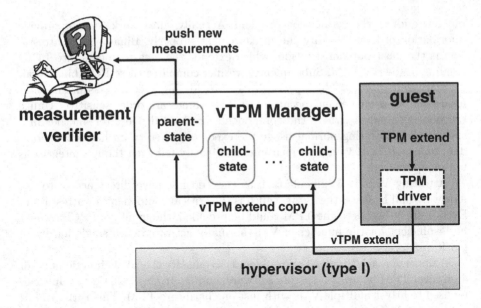

Fig. 5. Solution architecture in [11].

Another work [11] addresses the scalability issue by extending the vTPM model to reduce the complexity of software attestation. Since the traditional periodic polling model does not scale well (each VM adds effort to the attestation cost), the authors propose an event-based monitoring and pushing model. The benefit of the pushing model is that it will eliminate the problem of Time-of-Measure to Time-of-Report attacks and TPM reset attack (i.e. fast rebooting the system after the malicious script execution, to reset TPM PCR values).

The architecture proposed by the authors is shown in Fig. 5. The client TPM driver normally executes the TPM extend commands through the vTPM manager into its own child state. Now the vTPM manager can repeat the same extend operation into the parent state of the child state (which works like the PCRs in the hardware TPM). One parent state may create multiple child states, so that it can monitor multiple guest virtual machines at the same time. Every time the parent state is modified, the vTPM manager notifies the users that subscribe to it, thus achieving event-based attestation.

The obvious benefit for this solution is its scalability and the possibility to eliminate the ToM-ToR and TPM reset attacks. It can easily support thousands of VMs.

In general event-based monitoring is more convenient and feedback time can be much faster. In a virtualised environment, the hypervisor can be modified to support event-based monitoring. Following this idea, in [13] the authors propose to verify VM integrity by an *Integrity Verification Proxy (IVP)* embedded in the hypervisor. They chose QEMU/KVM as the hypervisor to be modified. The VMs running on top of KVM are in *Debug Mode*, so a debugging tool (e.g. **gdb**) can be used to set watchpoints (e.g. locations in memory) that are triggered by integrity-relevant operations such as Integrity Measurement Architecture (IMA) operations. Once the watchpoint is triggered, the VM will be paused and no outgoing/incoming traffic is possible. Until the module finishes to assess whether the new event violates an integrity criteria, the VM is not permitted to resume execution. This solution suffers a penalty due to executing the VMs in debug mode. Applying the same technique in normal mode is currently an open challenge.

3.2   IMA-Based Attestation

To support remote attestation in virtualised environment, the supporting component (SC) can be put in three different places (Fig. 6).

The first place is in the hosting system with a type II hypervisor.

The second option is to put it in a special VM (as done by vTPM). In this case, since the hosting system is not monitored, only a type I hypervisor can be used but neither the hypervisor nor the OS running in the VMs require modification.

The third option is to embed the supporting component within the hypervisor (either type I or type II) so that the supporting component can provide event-based attestation, but the hypervisor needs modification.

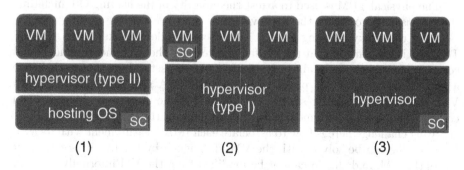

Fig. 6. Possible placement of the attestation supporting component.

We are currently exploring the first option: a remote attestation component running inside the hosting system underlying a type II hypervisor. This relies on the IMA measurements generated by the Linux kernel. It also requires a database of executable digests to show what software is running in the VMs and whether it is trusted or not. Since in SECURED the VM images are customised and their initial state is known, the only files that need to be checked are the configurations and the executable files loaded inside the VM.

The idea is to place one *attestation proxy* in the hosting system and use it to retrieve the IMA measurements from the VMs running inside it (Fig. 7). Since IMA measures all the executables invoked in VM, based on its policy, the IMA measurement is the key to ensure the integrity status of the VM.

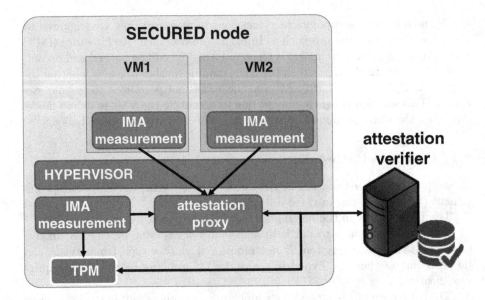

Fig. 7. IMA-based attestation architecture.

The physical TPM is used to attest the integrity of the hosting OS, including the attestation proxy and the hypervisor.

Since the proxy is doing what it is expected to do (thanks to the physical TPM), it is guaranteed that the verifier will retrieve the IMA measurements and compare them with its database. In this way, we can set a short time period (like a few seconds) to ask the proxy to retrieve the IMA measurements from each VM, and compute the digests of each of them. If the digest has changed, then compare the new measurement with the database in the verifier.

A big challenge here is how to associate each IMA measurement with its VM. Luckily, this can be solved with the VM-id assigned by the hypervisor when it starts the VM, and this id cannot be modified from the VM internally.

In order to improve the scalability, it is a good option to use the push model. So if the verifier detects that one VM integrity status is compromised (some unknown scripts were executed or some unknown configurations loaded), it can inform the attestation proxy which in turn can notify the user or simply shut down the VM.

4 Conclusions

SDN and NFV are useful technologies increasingly used to implement modern networking infrastructures. However, as they are heavily relying on various software components distributed by several actors, we need proper techniques to guarantee their trustworthiness and integrity. In this paper we have presented two possible approaches based on remote attestation to measure the integrity state of SDN switches and virtual machines executing critical network functions. However much more work is needed to solve practical issues (e.g. performance, management of cryptographic identity) as well as theoretical ones (e.g. fast and secure migration of VMs while maintaining their attestation state).

Acknowledgement. The research described in this paper is part of the SECURED project, co-funded by the European Commission (FP7 grant agreement no. 611458).

References

1. Dalton, C., Lioy, A., Lopez, D., Risso, F., Sassu, R.: Exploiting the network for securing personal devices. In: Cleary, F., Felic, M. (eds.) CSP Forum 2014. CCIS, vol. 470, pp. 16–27. Springer, Heidelberg (2014)
2. Open vSwitch. https://github.com/openvswitch/ovs
3. TrustedGRUB. http://sourceforge.net/projects/trustedgrub/
4. Sailer, R., Zhang, X., Jaeger, T., van Doorn, L.: Design and implementation of a TCG-based integrity measurement architecture. In: 13th USENIX Security Symposium, pp. 223–238, San Diego, 9–13 August 2004
5. ETSI NFV ISG: NFV Security / Problem Statement. Report ETSI GS NFV-SEC 001 (V1.1.1), October 2014. http://www.etsi.org/deliver/etsi_gs/NFV-SEC/001_099/001/01.01.01_60/gs_NFV-SEC001v010101p.pdf
6. ETSI NFV ISG: NFV Security / Security and Trust Guidance. Report ETSI GS NFV-SEC 003 (V1.1.1), December 2014. http://www.etsi.org/deliver/etsi_gs/NFV-SEC/001_099/003/01.01.01_60/gs_NFV-SEC003v010101p.pdf
7. ETSI NFV ISG: NFV / Use Cases. Report ETSI GS NFV 001 (V1.1.1), October 2013. http://www.etsi.org/deliver/etsi_gs/NFV/001_099/001/01.01.01_60/gs_NFV001v010101p.pdf
8. ETSI NFV ISG: NFV Proofs of Concept. http://www.etsi.org/technologies-clusters/technologies/nfv/nfv-poc
9. Jaeger, T., and Sailer, R., Shankar, U.: PRIMA: policy-reduced integrity measurement architecture. In: 11th ACM Symposium on Access Control Models and Technologies, pp. 19–28, Lake Tahoe, 7–9 June 2006
10. Berger, S., Sailer, R., Goldman, K.A.: vTPM: virtualizing the trusted platform module. In: 15th USENIX Security Symposium, Vancouver, pp. 305–320, Canada, July 31–August 8, 2006
11. Goldman, K., Sailer, R., Pendarakis, D., Srinivasan, D.: Scalable integrity monitoring in virtualized environments. In: 5th ACM Workshop on Scalable Trusted Computing, pp. 73–78, Chicago, 4–8 October 2010
12. Barham, P., Dragovic, B., Fraser, K., Hand, S., Harris, T., Ho, A., Neugebauer, R., Pratt, I., Warfield, A.: Xen and the art of virtualization. In: 19th ACM Symposium on Operating Systems Principles, pp. 164–177, Bolton Landing, 19–22 October 2003
13. Schiffman, J., Vijayakumar, H., Jaeger, T.: Verifying system integrity by proxy. In: Katzenbeisser, S., Weippl, E., Camp, L.J., Volkamer, M., Reiter, M., Zhang, X. (eds.) Trust 2012. LNCS, vol. 7344, pp. 179–200. Springer, Heidelberg (2012)

Research and Innovation in Cyber Security and Privacy

What's so Unique about Cyber Security?

Kenny Doyle[1(✉)], Zeta Dooly[1], and Paul Kearney[2]

[1] Telecommunications Software and Systems Group,
Waterford Institute of Technology, Waterford, Ireland
{kdoyle,zdooly}@tssg.org
[2] Security Research Centre, BT, London, UK
paul.3.kearney@bt.com

Abstract. The fields of Cyber Security and Privacy are among the fastest growing areas in technological development. With the increasing digitisation of key utilities and infrastructures, and the continuing exponential growth in the use of networked information and communications technologies (NICT) comes a concomitant growth in the need for security and privacy. While there are significant opportunities for profitable activity in these domains; the processes of innovation and garnering the requisite critical mass of users for a given system are fraught with difficulties some of which are unique to cyber security and privacy.

Keywords: Cyber security Privacy · Innovation · Threat agents · Optimal security systems

1 Introduction

The last three decades have seen exponential growth in the adoption of networked digital technologies. This growth encompasses many if not all of the key infrastructures which are crucial to the smooth running of much of global society. These key infrastructures include those of communication, finance and banking, utilities, as well as those which facilitate consumption, commerce, and entertainment. The interlinking of digital networks has been instrumental in the processes of the shrinking of time-space dimensions which in turn has been a key aspect in the attendant processes of globalisation. These developments have led to characterisations of contemporary advanced societies as being 'network societies' [1, 2] which are described by Castells in terms of being 'made up of networks of production, power and experience, which construct a culture of virtuality in the global flows that transcend time and space' [3].

While the benefits of network societies are apparent, there are significant risks and challenges which are products of the networked information age and have grown alongside these developments. Two of the main challenges are those which relate to privacy and security. The growth in the use of digital technologies and architectures has meant that there has been a rapid increase in the amount of data generated in a manner which is colloquially described as the data explosion. In 2010 Google CEO Eric Schmidt claimed that the amount of data produced in a two day period was equal to the total of all data generated from the dawn of mankind to the year 2003 [4]. A 2013 report by Sintef claimed that 90 % of global data at that time had been produced in the previous two years [5]. These statistics demonstrate how the data explosion has been

© Springer International Publishing Switzerland 2015
F. Cleary and M. Felici (Eds.): CSP Forum 2015, CCIS 530, pp. 131–139, 2015.
DOI: 10.1007/978-3-319-25360-2_11

vast, far reaching, and has occurred quickly with visible benefits in efficiencies, new knowledge, and innovations. Developments in the nascent fields of Big Data and the Internet of Things stand to further build upon, develop, and augment these trends.

The downsides of these developments are arguably as important yet less often fully understood as the benefits outlined above. Regulation in the hyper-connected, globalised world which has in many ways been facilitated by these technologies has been slow to catch up with the legal, social and political realities. Cybercrime under a variety of guises has been a concurrent feature of the developments described above; yet while criminals, hackers, and those out to disrupt networks operate in the global virtual 'space of flows' [6] those who are tasked with policing these networks operate according to national jurisdictions which are subject to legal, social and political rules, norms and laws which may constrain their efforts to operate effectively. These facts mean that developments in the field of cyber security should be prioritised as a means of protecting the structures of an increasingly networked world.

Practices of innovation in cyber security and privacy are in many ways different from those which are typical of other areas of technological development. The following sections will develop this point by describing the landscape of threat agents and elucidating the core principles of cyber security. It will then proceed to outline the aspects of cyber security developments which are unique and explain how these factors can act as an impediment to efficient and effective innovation in the field. It will then conclude with a brief description of an ideal type model of a system which balances the need for security with other important factors such as usability and cost. This paper aims to contribute to the literature on cyber security innovation by firstly offering a broad level description of threat agents, then offering a brief description of what will be termed principles of cyber security, and finally by describing some of the organisational challenges which may inhibit the realisation of these principles. This paper was compiled using extracts from the research outputs of both the IPACSO project [7–9] which is funded by the European Union under the FP7 framework program; and the NIS Platform Working Group 3 [10].

2   A Typology of Threat Agents

Recent years have witnessed the proliferation and diversification of classes of threat agent that are able and willing to exploit vulnerabilities for a variety of motives causing significant adverse impacts in the process. Unsurprisingly the most common motivation is financial, Europol have estimated that the global annual cost of cyber crime has reached €253 billion which makes it more profitable than the combined global trade in marijuana cocaine and heroin [11]. It would however be an over simplification to characterise all threat agents as being solely interested in financial gain. There are a range of threat agents who break into and disrupt the operations of networks and systems for varying reasons which will now be examined and described. This list is by no means exhaustive and the reason for the inclusion of these particular threat agents is primarily that of the fact that they have been involved in recent incidents which have been widely reported on in the international media. The threat landscape is one which is evolvable and so the range of threat actors is ever increasing.

2.1 Hackers

The phrase 'hacker' is one which subject to contestation and means different things according to different people. In the 1960's the term hacker was 'a positive label used to describe someone who was highly skilled in developing creative, elegant and effective solutions to computing problems' [12]. More recent definitions of hackers are associated with illegal and even criminal activities of breaking into secure systems with the intention of stealing data or even just to disrupt the service or to deface a website. The motivations for hacking vary from financial gain, to disrupting the operation of systems as a means of demonstrating technical expertise, to gaining social capital or prestige amongst counter-cultural peer groups. Hacking as a means of political protest has also become increasingly popular spawning the phrase 'hacktivism' in the process [13]. The act of hacking is thus often defined by the purpose for which it is carried out; some of these examples will now be examined.

2.2 Criminal Hackers

While most acts of gaining entry to systems without permission are illegal many hobbyist hackers do so for reasons which do not involve using this act of primary deviance as a means of committing further criminal acts. Hobbyist hackers like those mentioned above refer to criminal hackers as 'crackers' and reject their practices of hacking for the purposes of committing crime. In common parlance however this distinction goes unrecognised and the words hacker and cracker are synonymous. When hacking is carried out with the intention of stealing sensitive data which can be used to commit crimes such as identity theft or blackmail it can be constituted as criminal hacking. Sensitive data could include financial or personal details which could be used for the purpose of identity theft.

While these data may be acquired by breaking into systems or by utilising technological expertise, a key point of note is that 'hacking' in this sense can also denote forms of blagging or spoofing. These are forms of manipulation which happen without the use of sophisticated technology and are more akin to psychological tricks of misdirection and deception. Social engineering or human hacking [14] as it is sometimes called involves targeted deception which involves tricking people into giving out information which can be used profitably. The conception of cyber security as a technological problem which may only be solved by technological means is thus problematic when these factors are considered.

A further aspect of criminal hacking is that criminal groups have become involved in the design and distribution of tools which can be used to carry out attacks by anyone who has the means to use them. This means that the ability to commit disruptive criminal cyber attacks has been functionally democratised. An example of this can be seen with programs like LOIC –Low Orbit Ion Cannon- which can be used for denial of service (DOS) and distributed denial of service (DDOS) attacks. LOIC is an open source software which was used most notably by the hacker group Anonymous in their attacks on the church of Scientology in an act which they defined as hacktivism [15].

2.3   State Sponsored Hacker Groups

As well as these types there are also groups which are organised with plausible deniability by established and on the face of it reputable institutional actors such as Transnational Corporations or even Nation States. These groups can be used for activities such as espionage, data theft, or disruption of service attacks which will further the aims of the parent organisation. Examples of such groups include the 'APT28' group who were allegedly acting on behalf of the Russian government [16] and the 'Axiom' group who allegedly operate at the behest of the Chinese government [17]. The most famous example of such an operation in recent history is that of the 'stuxnet' virus which disrupted and delayed the uranium enrichment program of Iran. Actions such as this are indicative of how the realm of cyber space has come to be characterised by military strategists in terms of being the fifth domain of warfare after land, sea, air, and space [18].

2.4   The Insider Threat

A further addition to this list is that of the insider threat which is a prevalent yet under resourced element of security. 'Research indicates that 70 % of fraud is perpetrated by insiders rather than by external criminals but that 90 % of security controls and monitoring are focused on external threats' [19]. While many off the shelf security products are useful for detecting and blocking outsider intrusion into a network, it is unfeasible for such solely technological solutions to be effective against insiders who often may need access to parts of the network to carry out their day to day work. The unique aspect of the insider threat is that such threat agents often have legitimate access as well as intimate knowledge and expertise in using the system they are attacking. This ensures that they have the means and the knowledge to inflict the greatest amount of damage while leaving the least amount of evidence behind making them a particularly pernicious and insidious risk. The term "insider" is usually used to describe someone with legitimate access to an organisation's assets and who abuses that access to commit an unauthorised act. Insider incidents may be perpetrated deliberately or accidentally and may even be unwitting, where an employee may be recruited, coerced, or duped into committing an unauthorised act on someone else's behalf [20].

Economic and organisational developments such as outsourcing have inadvertently increased the risk of insider threats. This is due to the fact that when an operation is outsourced it becomes subject to the security standards of more than one organisation. This can mean that security standards can become fragmented and diluted with more people having access to the system. A security system is only as secure as the weakest link in its chain, and where some operations are outsourced it can be the case that security standards are relaxed as they become geographically dispersed and more difficult to enforce.

The insider threat includes employees or former employees who may have a grievance with the organisation and so wish to cause embarrassment; or it could just as easily include employees who disagree with aspects of the organisations' activities and wish to publicise them by becoming whistle blowers. Insider incidents can also happen by accident where a user inadvertently releases information or allows outside access if they are the victims of social engineering. Insider threat agents are often the most effective at gaining access or causing disruption to a system and are thus often targeted by outsiders as a means of access either by coercion or manipulation.

3   Elucidating Cyber Security: Key Principles

Following on from the description of the range of threat agents it can be seen that cyber security involves combat with an intelligent foe. Rather than being about solving a static problem, it is an adversarial 'game' between attack and defence. On a tactical level, the 'game' is about preventing and responding to attacks, while on a strategic level it is about co-evolution of tools and tactics. This makes the future threat environment highly dynamic and extremely difficult to predict. In consequence, security solutions need be continuously evolvable in order to establish and maintain a lead over the threat without leaving windows of vulnerability. Furthermore, the number, diversity, organisation, persistence and sophistication of threat agents facing the defender is continually growing, with some having a high degree of expertise, organisation, motivation, persistence and financial and political backing. As described above with the functional democratisation of hacking technologies; even amateur threat agents have easy access to powerful, automated attack tools.

As well as this attackers will probe defences to find and exploit any weak link meaning that solutions must be recognised as complex human-technical systems consisting of many dissimilar elements that must work together harmoniously. Consequently they require a holistic approach. Currently, technical security measures are largely used independently, with people providing the matrix that integrates the components. In the future, the pace of response required means that the technical systems will need to co-operate directly. This has implications for the dynamics of innovation as it is more difficult for a radically different approach to penetrate the market due to the need for a new product or service to be compatible with the existing elements with which it must interact.

Cyber Security is not a technology itself, but a mind-set and a collection of principles that must be applied in a technical and organisational/social context. In an organisational sense this should manifest itself in terms of a culture of security, where all members of the organisation are informed and motivated to ensure security of informational assets. As outlined above such a culture must move beyond merely technological solutions and must encompass behavioural aspects at both the level of the individual and the organisation. To be effective such a culture must be robust and consistent while remaining unobtrusive so it does not hinder productivity.

The pace of innovation in technology and in the business practices, leisure activities and societal institutions that exploit it, means that cyber security must re-invent itself continuously. As well as this it is important to outline the social, political and regulatory aspects of the cyber security technologies and developments. As end-users are becoming increasingly aware of some of the privacy aspects of networked information and communications technologies they are also beginning to alter their behaviour and to demand higher levels of privacy and security of their personal information. These demands can range from avoiding the use of products or services which are seen to have lax standards, to lobbying regulators to enforce higher standards via compulsory instruments. This means that the regulatory environment in cyber security and privacy is a changeable landscape which can at any time be subject to new regulations and demands. Due to this fact it is a necessary condition that privacy and cyber security systems be agile, adaptable and amenable to change in the face of new threats, new demands from end users and new requirements from regulators and legislators.

4 Barriers to Cyber Security Innovation

Innovation can be crucial to the success and even survival of many organisations. Processes of effective innovation are by definition risky enterprises to be undertaken. Innovation is both costly and time consuming and never comes with any guarantee of success or return on investment; yet the alternative of ignoring innovation would ensure that an organisation is static in a changeable world. While there are universal barriers to innovation such as cost and risk avoidance, in the field of cyber security and privacy there are a unique set of factors which can restrict effective innovation. Some of these factors which are possibly unique to cyber security and privacy will now be examined.

4.1 Trust Related Barriers to Entry

Research indicates that trust is a core factor in the field of cyber security [21], any organisation which is in the market for such products must be able to trust the service providers. Potential buyers of cyber security and privacy products and solutions are unlikely to advertise or discuss weaknesses in their ICT architecture. This understandable reticence is due to the fact that they do not wish to make disclosures which could lead to threats to their business. An offshoot of this is that PACS innovation market research and needs analyses are difficult to conduct which raises barriers to market entry for new organisations. These reasons also make it difficult to elicit technical requirements from potential users of security products. End-users will not openly disclose requirements with anyone that doesn't have existing contacts in the domain, evidence of security credentials, or established reference customers. Buyers will essentially stay away from those without an established trusted relationship with them, or with others in the marketplace.

4.2 High Start- up Costs

The issues of trust identified above are also related to start- up costs, creating a trusted security product will be expensive. Start-up costs for cyber-security innovators are higher than they are for those operating in other technological domains. Some of the typically higher costs include those of infrastructure which must be met upfront, as well as high testing and product certification costs. The development process for security products and services involves long consultative sales cycles that impact heavily on operating cash flow; and heavy investment in R&D is needed to sustain product roadmaps and keep them relevant in line with ever-changing technologies and threats.

These costs can combine to make it prohibitively expensive for SME's and start-up companies to enter the market even if they have a feasible and achievable idea.

4.3 Regulatory Landscape

The field of cyber security and privacy is one which is highly influenced and structured by legal and regulatory actors. Within each region there are a set of policy guidelines and legal regulations which tangibly structure the end product. In the EU for example there are regulations which range from the Data Protection Directives, to the Cookie Directive and the Network and Information Society (NIS) Directive. In the US there are the Federal Information Security Amendments Acts, as well as the Do-Not-Track-Online act to name but two examples. As well as regulatory instruments such as these there are also national and regional laws which will be influential in determining the operation of the end product of security development. Such laws and regulations are malleable and are likely to be influenced by social and political events. There are often public calls for changes in regulations in response to large scale public events such as data loss or a high profile security breach. Such regulatory changes can fundamentally alter the operation of a security system and so must always be considered at the design stage.

4.4 Creating a Compelling Argument for Return on Investment

Convincing potential buyers of the need for security systems and justifying the return on investment can be difficult. In the strictest sense they are not direct creators of value and instead can be characterised as systems which can prevent and assuage potential losses. While the costs may be severe in terms of either financial or reputational loss after the event; it can be difficult to convince potential buyers of the need to be protected against intangible, potential losses. As well as this it is not usually possible to tell how many times a security system has protected a network, or to financially quantify the level that prevented losses would amount to. Thus when dealing within the constraints of limited resources, many IT systems buyers will choose to invest in systems which can directly create financial value instead of systems which will insure against potential losses. These factors do not constitute an exhaustive list, yet when combined they demonstrate some of what is unique about innovation in the field of cyber security.

5 Optimal Model for Cyber Security Systems

A further aspect of cyber security technologies which is unique relates to the process of making purchasing decisions. Such decisions regarding security systems can be characterised in terms of being a balancing act. The system must be as secure as possible but within the bounds of reasonable cost; the system must be robust, but also easy to update in the face of a fluid and changeable threat landscape which is always capable of producing unforeseen eventualities. As has been alluded to above security systems bring with them many benefits which are difficult to measure and so communicating the importance of investment in security is not a straightforward proposition.

As is the case with a decision to purchase insurance, it is the case that organisations are most likely to decide to invest in security systems directly after a breach has occurred. This type of reactive purchasing strategy has obvious limitations in as far as it is reacting to an event that has already happened and by which stage the damage is already done. The obverse of this is a proactive purchasing strategy which attempts to second guess what form future risks to security will take. While from the standpoint of security the proactive strategy is better than the reactive, it comes with an important caveat which relates to cost. If a system is designed in an attempt to protect against all conceivable threats then it is likely that much of these threats will never materialise and so there will be redundancies in the system. From the buyer perspective these redundancies are paid for using funds which are limited and could be better employed elsewhere. So in making purchasing decisions for a security system it is essential to balance the cost of potential security breaches with the cost of security measures as beyond this point any increases in security expenditures are redundant [22].

6 Conclusion

The importance of effective cyber security to wider society cannot be overstated; core infrastructures such as utilities and communications are increasingly becoming digitised. This means that cyber security is not just about protecting the informational assets of companies or nation states but instead is about protecting many of the key infrastructures upon which we rely. This paper began by describing the importance of developments in effective cyber security solutions, and then proceeded to outline a typology of threat agents. The following two sections aimed to elucidate the reasons why cyber security is a unique field of technological development. Cyber security differs from many other fields of technological development for a number of reasons. It is an adversarial exchange between security actors and threat agents such as those outlined above, and security requirements can change very quickly according to the dictates of social, political and economic events. This means that in terms of design, effective security systems must be agile and easy to update and change while simultaneously being robust and secure. Despite its importance in the future of our networked world it is also a technology for which financial justification can be difficult due to the fact of many of its utilities not being amenable to capture by standardised metrics of worth.

References

1. Castells, M.: The Rise of the Network Society. Blackwell Publishers Inc., Oxford (2000)
2. Van Dijk, J.: The Network Society: Social Aspects of New Media. Sage Publications Ltd., London (2005)

3. Castells, M.: End of the Millennium, p. 370. Blackwell Publishers Inc., Oxford (1998)
4. Whelan, E., Teigland, R.: Managing information overload: examining the role of the human filter (2010). SSRN 1718455
5. Sintef Big Data, for better or worse: 90 % of world's data generated over last two years. Science Daily (2013)
6. Europol. https://www.europol.europa.eu/ec/cybercrime-growing
7. IPACSO Innovation Framework for ICT Security Deliverable D2.2, Market and Regulatory Environment & Industry Analysis Report (2014)
8. IPACSO Innovation Framework for ICT Security Deliverable D2.3 PACS Technology and Research Spectrum Report (2014)
9. Jentzsch, N.: IPACSO Innovation Framework for ICT Security Deliverable D4.1 State-of-the-art of the Economics of Cyber security and Privacy (2014)
10. Kearney, P., Dooly, Z. (eds.): NIS Platform Working Group 3 (WG3) Business Cases and Innovation Paths (2014)
11. Castells, M.: The Rise of the Network Society. Blackwell Publishers Inc., Oxford (2000)
12. Yar, M.: Cybercrime and Society. Sage Publications Ltd., London (2006)
13. Steinmetz, K., Gerber, J.: It doesn't have to be this way: hacker perspectives on privacy. Soc. Justice **41**(3), 29–51 (2015)
14. Mann, I.: Hacking the Human: Social Engineering Techniques and Security Countermeasures. Ashgate Publishing, Aldershot (2008)
15. Sauter, M.: LOIC will tear us apart : the impact of tool design and media portrayals in the success of activist DDOS Attacks. Am. Behav. Sci. **57**(7), 983–1007 (2013)
16. Fox-Brewster, T.: 'State sponsored' Russian hacker group linked to cyber attacks on neighbours. The Guardian London (2014)
17. Stone, J.: China-Backed Hacking Group Axiom Said to Have Attacked 43,000 Computers. International Business Times USA (2014)
18. Murphy, M.: War in the fifth domain. Economist (2010). http://www.economist.com/node/16478792
19. Fyffe, G.: Addressing the insider threat. Netw. Secur. **3**, 11–14 (2008)
20. Colwill, C.: Human factors in information security: the insider threat – who can you trust these days? Inf. Secur. Tech. Rep. **14**(4), 186–196 (2009)
21. IPACSO D2.2, Market and Regulatory Environment & Industry Analysis Report (2014)
22. Jentzcsh, N.: IPACSO Innovation Framework for ICT Security Deliverable D4.1. Market and Regulatory Environment & Industry Analysis Report (2015)

Uncovering Innovation Practices and Requirements in Privacy and Cyber Security Organisations: Insights from IPACSO

Zeta Dooly[1,2], Kenny Doyle[1], and Jamie Power[2(✉)]

[1] Waterford Institute of Technology, TSSG, Waterford, Ireland
zdooly@tssg.org, kdoyle@wit.ie
[2] Waterford Institute of Technology, RIKON, Waterford, Ireland
jrpower@wit.ie

Abstract. A pressing challenge facing the cybersecurity and privacy research community is transitioning technical R&D into commercial and marketplace ready products and services. Responding to the need to develop a better understanding of how Privacy and CyberSecurity (PACS) market needs and overall technology innovation best-practice can be harmonized more effectively the contribution of this paper is centred upon uncovering PACS stakeholders' innovation practices, requirements, and challenges and in doing so highlighting scope for innovation intervention supports. The research outputs impacts and has implications at various levels, most notably in terms of framing both innovator and firm-level innovation requirements within the PACS domain, which has relevance to academic and policy making audiences also. Additionally, given that the research outputs form a pivotal component of the IPACSO project, they will actively contribute to ongoing debates and objectives around shaping support measures for PACS innovation awareness, competency building and innovation policy support developments in the domain.

Keywords: Innovation · Requirements · Challenges · Privacy · Cybersecurity

1 Introduction and Research Focus Rationale

The publication of the EU CyberSecurity Strategy [1] coupled with Europe 2020 strategy and its flagship initiatives such as The Innovation Union and Digital Agenda all underscore the escalating importance of innovation. Reflective of this, opportunities for innovators in the privacy and cybersecurity domain is increasing. Nonetheless, challenges of transitioning technology related research developments and outputs to real-world deployment are well documented. Nonetheless, a range of challenges including, but not limited to: pursuing a narrow innovation process failing to incorporate the internal and external ecosystem or customer needs, an overemphasis on technology-driven bottom-up innovation, in addition to unsupportive deployment channels for research output/commercialization's hamper the transitioning of technology related research developments and outputs to commercial deployment [2].

A pressing challenge facing the cybersecurity and privacy research community is transitioning technical R&D into commercial and marketplace ready products and

© Springer International Publishing Switzerland 2015
F. Cleary and M. Felici (Eds.): CSP Forum 2015, CCIS 530, pp. 140–150, 2015.
DOI: 10.1007/978-3-319-25360-2_12

services – "New and innovative technologies will only make a difference if they are deployed and used. It does not matter how visionary a technology is unless it meets the needs and requirements of customers/users and it is available as a product via channels that are acceptable to the customers/users" [2]. While innovation is widely recognized by industry and academics as a sustainable and competitive enabler, nonetheless understanding of innovation management and practice remains fragmented, misunderstood and untamed by practitioners and researchers [3, 4]. Innovation practice and requirements are far from straightforward *"...most innovation is messy, involving false starts, recycling between stages, dead ends and jumps out of sequence"* [10]. Varying attempts have been made to articulate conceptual order on the innovation processes of organisations, in the form of innovation process models and the variety amongst the models is the consequence of a lack of consensus as to how an innovation process should look like, given the unique requirements, contexts, environments, and purposes for which they are developed [10, 11]. Indeed, several authors acknowledge that innovation process does not occur within a vacuum, and thereby indicate a range of contextual factors which impact on the processes deployed [12–15]. Such contextual factors range from organisational characteristics to societal factors and from influenceable factors to external factors.

Innovators operate within complex and turbulent environments, and are increasingly confronted with escalating and rapid technology developments, competitive global market competition and shorter product life cycles meaning they must be reactive and flexible to organizational, technological and market shifts [5]. Indeed, the privacy and cybersecurity market is deeply influenced from various themes driven by technical, human, societal, organizational, economic, legal, and regulatory concerns among others; these factors combine to create marketplace and innovation ecosystem with complex value chain relationships [6]. Innovation therefore cannot not occur within a vacuum and is impacted upon by a range of external contextual factors in addition to the following internal considerations, including but not limited to, strategy and culture, resources and skills, leadership, organizational structure and external linkages [7–9]. Reflective of the above, innovation practice is far from straightforward *"...most innovation is messy, involving false starts, recycling between stages, dead ends and jumps out of sequence"* [3].

Mindful of this, through a specific PACS lens, IPACSO aims to support innovators in both industry and research communities with a responsive innovation framework to enhance their overall innovation engagement, management and deployment activities. IPACSO is an EU-funded Coordination and Support Action (CSA) project aimed at supporting Privacy and CyberSecurity innovations in Europe - www.ipacso.eu. IPACSO is focused on adapting existing innovation methodologies available in other domains, both general and specific; optimizing these approaches for the Privacy and CyberSecurity (PACS) market domains. The research outputs impacts and has implications at various levels, most notably in terms of framing both innovator and firm-level innovation requirements with reference to informing the IPACSO framework. Additionally, given that the research outputs form a pivotal component of the IPACSO project, they will actively contribute to ongoing debates and objectives around shaping support and policy measures for PACS innovation awareness, competency building and innovation policy support developments in the domain.

2 Research Methodology

In pursuit of identifying PACS stakeholders' innovation requirements a small-scale mixed method triangulated research design was employed, encompassing an online questionnaire, semi-structured telephone interviews and secondary desk research. Derived from IPACSO's overarching stakeholder focus, two key categories of interest formed the target sampling frame; specifically innovators and enablers. "**Innovators**": individuals or companies that are looking to bring ideas in the PACs domain to market. Sub-categories include researchers, vendors, service providers, integrators and infrastructure providers. "**Enablers**": individuals or entities who are responsible for supporting individuals or companies in being more innovative and in commercialising technology. The research respondents included IPACSO members, Innovation Advisory Board Members, NIS WG3 members amongst other individuals and organisations engaged with through IPACSO exploitation and dissemination events.

This triangulated research design approach enabled for multiple sources of data to be collected and integrated in pursuit of documenting stakeholders' innovation requirements and enhancing the reliability and validity of the subsequent analysis. The survey design, which consisted of ranking and open ended questions was informed from the Community Innovation Survey guide and was administered online via SurveyMonkey. A semi-structured interview guide was developed in parallel to the survey instrument.

Reflecting IPACSO's multi-stakeholder foci, a broad range of stakeholder categories are represented in the research findings ranging from industry innovators in the PACS domain, research innovators, innovation intermediaries in the form of consultancy and industry support, in addition to funding and policy representatives. PACS relevant subdomains of those who participated in the research include but are not limited to: mobile and cloud security, telco, cyber protection, cryptography, malware, privacy enhancing technologies, surveillance and intrusion detection, security intelligence, distributed computing and big data. Regarding organisation size, categories ranging from micro to large are represented with small organisations (34.8 %) leading the response rate followed by micro (26.1 %) and large (26.1 %) and medium size organisations (13 %) respectively. The data reflects the growing consensus of small enterprises proliferating the diverse and fragmented PACS landscape, with small and micro firms accounting for over half of all participants in the research. Demonstrating a diverse canvas of participation from all areas within organisational structures, respondents included: founders and directors, R&D managers and personnel, CTO's, commercial directors and business developers, CEO's, project and product managers, technology transfer managers, professors and researchers from research institutes, policy makers and security evangelists.

3 Research Findings

This research findings are focused on the innovation practice of PACS stakeholders, in the context of the innovation value chain, and serves to provide requirements and scenario inputs to inform the development of the IPACSO Innovation Framework. For this reason, the primary research investigation focused on identifying stakeholders innovation scenarios, practices and requirements to develop an understanding of the following:

- Stakeholders' innovation practices, including current environment, approaches and requirements in relation to innovation engagement.
- Challenges, barriers and support requirements in relation to PACS innovation.

3.1 Innovation Practices

A diverse approach to organising innovation transcends the practices of the study's respondents. In terms of identifying innovation practices, this section reports on the respondents' innovation foci, means for organizing innovation, stakeholder involved and self-rated competency levels.

The majority of observable innovation in cyber-security and privacy markets is best described as incremental. This means that much of the innovation is a product or service improvement, but not a radically new development that forces businesses to re-organization or leads to the emergence of wholly new markets. For instance, a responding Telco organisation identified that given their positioning in the middle of the supply chain, their innovations are incremental in terms of integrating components of technology from suppliers, tech plug-ins for a platform or providing a service wrap around technology deliver. In a similar vein, a software services, devices and solutions company reported that that they do not produce many classic cyber security products. Instead, they strive that cyber security is built in to products and services as their customers expect that what they deliver is secure. In terms of the respondents to this study product and service innovation dominate their primary innovation focus; whereas process innovation represents the key secondary focus. Conversely, organisational and marketing innovation was not reported as a focus by 50 % and 40 % of respondents respectively.

Two thirds of respondents adopt a cross functional approach to facilitate innovation; whereas a third utilize specialized organization units (e.g. research centres). Of note, over a quarter of respondents reported an ad-hoc, informal approach to innovation organisation and a further 16.7 % identified that their innovation operations are conducted externally through outsourcing arrangements. Demonstrating that innovation practice is a combination of technology push and demand pull dimensions, both of these categories are strongly represented amongst the respondents. Reflecting the previously reported dominant role of internal cross functional staff integration, a cooperative and parallel approach is also commonly pursued. Indicating a potential lack of innovation governance, only one in in five respondents reported a stage gated process. Underscoring the escalating incidences of collaborations between innovating organisations and external stakeholders, over 50 % positive agreement statements were reported for systems/networking integration and open innovation models. A wide-ranging spectrum of stakeholders were reported to be involved in innovation activities, albeit at varying levels. Internal staff represent the highest frequency of stakeholders used, followed by a combination of clients/customers, competitors, consultants are utilised at lower levels of frequency with professional/industry associations, universities and government/research institutes being used as less frequent partners. A significant proportion of respondents indicated that external stakeholders such as suppliers, competitors and consultants are never involved in the innovation processes or activities within their organisation.

Innovation competency levels amongst the respondents varied across the innovation value chain; indeed, the respondents identified high and competent levels of proficiency is the areas of ideation and concept development and design and business analysis. Nonetheless, it was still reported that ideation and business analysis phases lacked systematic and comprehensive attention. On a more positive note, almost 80 % of respondents identified that their development processes are flexible enough to be adapted to market conditions and project reports. Over half of responses identified that lean and agile approaches are followed for innovation development. Regarding the concluding aspect of the innovation process, i.e. the launch, less than half of respondents utilize a multi-disciplinary team approach to ensure their innovation outputs are targeted, launched and delivered to the marketplace. Areas where respondents felt there was scope for improvement included the phases towards the end of the lifecycle including test, implementation and post launch.

3.2   Innovation Challenges

This section synopsized the innovation challenges, barriers and pain-points identified by the respondents to the study. Specifically, the respondents were asked to rate how the following typical innovation challenges related to their organisation. The typical innovation challenges included:

- Infrastructure Factors (e.g. lack of innovation governance, inadequate innovation management procedures, ad-hoc R&D practices, lack of collaborative structures etc.);
- Cost Factors (e.g. lack of appropriate funds within the enterprise/from external sources, innovation costs too high etc.);
- Knowledge Factors (e.g. lack of qualified personnel, limited information on markets, difficulty in finding cooperation partners etc.);
- Market Factors (e.g. market dominated by established enterprises, uncertain demand for goods and services etc.);
- Legal and Regulatory Factors (e.g. escalating legislative and regulatory requirements).

As presented in Fig. 1, variance was reported across all categories of challenge factors. Unsurprisingly, cost factors came first for all the respondents with a score in the region of 70 %. One out of five respondents also identified knowledge and market factors as a serious problematic innovation challenge. A significant finding is that all of the challenge factors rated as both moderate and minor challenges for the respondents.

Elaborating upon these findings, Table 1 below synopsizes a range of related and additional challenges which impede undertaking innovation in the PACS context. Replicating the findings in Fig. 1 above, cost, regulatory, infrastructure and market forces are represented, in addition to business knowledge, threats, awareness and acceptance challenges.

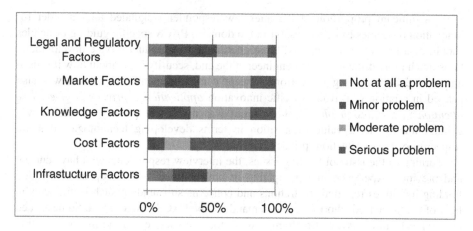

Fig. 1. Innovation challenges

Table 1. Innovation barriers in PACS

Human (skills, intelligence, availability)	Very high expertise of internal resources. Access to the right developers with specialised competence/Skilled resources. Idea implementers. Staff shortages
Funding/resources	Financial resources/funding (we operate 100 % on cash flow). Cost of development. Competing internal resources
Policies/procedures	Internal practices. Common policies missing. IPR and patent landscaping
Market issues	Competitiveness between collaborators. Market positioning issues
Regulation	Regulatory barriers. Navigating the minefield. Stumbling block. Detect, block and clean new malware
Business Knowledge	Business modelling. Underpinning business case. Diffusion and route to market
Awareness and Acceptance	Acceptance of new technology concepts. Education in privacy enhancing technologies
Top management	Corporate engagement and involvement

While market shifts and demands represent a key innovation component and driven in any industry setting, the constantly changing and hard to predict PACS environment exerts a significant challenge. Interview respondents were in agreement that the speed of innovation and short product cycles are signature aspects of digital markets which are continuously altered through emerging threat and vulnerabilities "it's a continuous race between hackers and solution, the target is always moving and so too is the risk". The analogy of a Knight in a Suit of Armour was used to describe the imperative of being able to move and fight in terms of innovation engagement. Equally so, it was cautioned that research, innovation and development priorities cannot be solely based on today's problem – the world moves on, new waves of technology and threats are emerging, the key is finding windows of opportunity.

A significant proportion of the interview respondents signaled that in order for innovation outcomes to be successful in the domain, PACS specific guiding principles should be a motivator, as opposed to an afterthought of product/service development. "It is much more difficult to retro-engineer at the end, security is all about how it is used and should be a driving force from concept commencement". This point was also echoed in relation to privacy specific innovation applications *"privacy is given little attention in the design phase"*; however it was noted that privacy by design was gaining traction as a value proposition in terms developing technologies that are respectful of data protection, privacy legislation.

Turning to the issue of funding issues, the interview respondents who have current and previous experience of participating in both national and European innovation funding initiatives reported frustrations and concerns surrounding such instruments in light of the fast paced, short lifecycle demands of the PACS environment. Some argued the typical three year timeframe was too restrictive in terms of getting products/solutions to close to market stage; whereas others argued that projects should be longer to accommodate the early stages of the innovation value chain lifecycle. It was recognised that with the advent of Horizon 2020, concentrated efforts were being mobilized to facilitate more agile innovation activities and a broader spectrum of funding criteria with reference to innovation actions.

3.3 Innovation Requirements

Advancing upon the identification of the respondents innovation practices and challenges, this section reports upon their requirements with reference to supporting and accelerating innovation engagement and practice.

Echoing the WEF fostering innovation report [16] which categories entrepreneurship driven innovation into three categories – stand up, start up, scale up – the level of innovation requirements of innovators varies depending on their respective maturity level. For instance, respondents from MNCs (Multinational Corporation) identified that broad, complex and highly structured innovation ecosystems, departments, policies and strategies are a hallmark of their organisations. Such infrastructures accordingly facilitate a complex web of innovation activities both internally and externally encompassing industrial applied research projects, technology driven research and collaboration with other companies and research institutes/universities. The reported positives of such an environment included the access of multi-disciplinary support from internal stakeholders to develop both technical and business case advances. It was reported that large MNC operations have dedicated resources, facilities and manpower to consistently and systematically scan for external innovations that may be capable of exploitation. Examples include: monitoring start-ups, incubators/labs, competitions for SMES, Hothouse Brainstorming sessions, funding research programmes centres in universities, collaboration with SMEs. Equally so, negatives were reported in relation to an overly bureaucratic, stage-gated innovation environment and infrastructure with reference to research project lags versus short time market opportunities *"Frameworks are difficult too – they can be a straitjacket or an enabler"*. Conversely, small scale start-up respondents reported that their relative infancy in terms of maturity restricted their capacity to implement and deploy defined and structured innovation systems; largely due to financial, manpower and access to networking constraints – *"...if you are a start-up you need to factor in overheads to go through a process. Often start-ups favour getting bought up by larger companies in order to fully realise and exploit their idea/concept"*.

When questioned about innovation areas/aspects where they consider support, guidance and knowledge would be of benefit the respondents highlighted a range of requirements and scope for opportunities. Figure 2 presents the results, and indicates essential and high priorities across the board in all of the areas with between 25 % - 65 % of respondents. Strong requirements for innovation supports were reported in the areas of portfolio management, post launch, resource and competence management and business intelligence.

Elaborating upon these findings, Table 2 synopsizes a range of related and additional innovation requirement areas, in terms of areas presenting scope for improvement. Replicating the findings in Fig. 2 above, cost, market, human and business intelligence are strongly priority in addition to calls for networking, collaboration and innovation/risk awareness building.

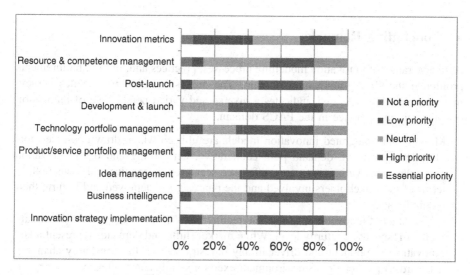

Fig. 2. Scope for innovation supports

A common denominator from the interview findings is the varying levels of disconnect between research and technology development and innovation diffusion/ implementation. While the imperative of underpinning innovation development activities with sound commercial business cases was recognised by all, competency and proficiency in this area varies significantly. This was particularly pronounced in an interview with a business development manager within a university cyber security research group – *"....commercial validation, demand and risk is not well understood by researchers; technologists don't focus on intricacies of business modelling or marketplace risk"*.

Table 2. Additional Scope for Innovation Supports

Economic Supports	Funding of expensive projects; EU/Government incentives in innovation (Tax incentives); Economic assistance and investment supports.
Networking and Collaboration supports	Assistance in linking with major companies; Programmes to encourage smaller and larger companies to collaborate.
Market Supports	Regulation screening and patent searching; Targeted initiatives aimed at channel development; Assistance in scanning the market; Resources for market knowledgebase identification, needs identification.
Human/People supports	Top management commitment; Access to key competence for hiring; dedicated training and consultancy supports.
Business Development Supports	Market positioning; Marketing; Business intelligence; PR; Implementation and customer engagement; Benchmarking.
Risk and Awareness Building Supports	Initiatives for encouraging disruptive innovation engagement; Confidence building in ideation and follow through; Initiatives to promote European enterprises to be leaders as opposed to followers.

4 Concluding Remarks

A diverse range of innovation modelling processes, practices and, in turn, requirements proliferate the PACS innovation domain. The analysis, which triangulates survey, interview and desk research, indicates a diverse and varied perspective of innovation organisation and practice in the PACS domain.

Multiple and integrated innovation models are utilised which draw upon elements of technology push, demand pull, cooperative, networking and open innovation principles. This variance, creates difference scenarios of practice and focus both in terms of the stakeholders involved and the phases/gates deployed and in turn, their requirements.

The level of innovation practice and requirements of innovators varies depending on their respective maturity level. While market shifts and demands represent a key innovation component and driver in any industry setting, the constantly changing and hard to predict PACS environment exerts a significant challenge.

At a high level, the research indicates that existing competencies and investment are directed in the early phases of the innovation lifecycle (ideation through to concept development); whereas significant scope and requirements occur in the latter stages (test and implementation). A significant finding is that innovation challenges transcend infrastructural, market, knowledge, cost and legal domains. Cost factors came first for all the respondents with knowledge and market factors also representing a serious problematic innovation challenge.

The stakeholders identified a broad scope for innovation supports across the entire innovation value chain and ecosystem (i.e. strategy, business intelligence, ideation, portfolio management, resource management development, and launch).

A common denominator from the interview findings is the varying levels of disconnect between research and technology development and innovation diffusion/implementation. While the imperative of underpinning innovation development activities with sound commercial business cases was recognized by all, competency and proficiency in this area varies significantly.

Turning to recommendations gleaned from the analysis, cognizance is taken of the small-scale nature of the research and its project-specific purpose; nonetheless, the research outputs impacts and has implications at various levels, most notably in terms of framing both innovator and firm-level innovation requirements within the PACS domain, which has relevance to PACS policy making audiences also. Additionally, given that the research outputs form a pivotal component of the IPACSO project, they will actively contribute to ongoing debates and objectives around shaping support measures for PACS innovation awareness, competency building and innovation policy support developments in the domain.

For innovators - it is pertinent to note that there is no one size fits all solution to designing and implementing a successful innovation process as each innovation ecosystem and value chain needs to be aligned to its respective organisational context. Nonetheless, there is an ever increasing general body of information around innovation practice and modelling which has direct relevance to informing firm-level innovation practice: i.e. the set of rules, models and stages involved; considerations for R&D, utilizing both internal and external knowledge sources/collaborators and responding to market forces and the strengths and weaknesses of the various generations of innovation models.

For policy makers and enablers – the analysis highlights the importance of the need to integrate the innovation ecosystem (internal and external) and consider the various stages of the innovation lifecycle/value chain in terms of supporting and cultivating end-to-end innovation activities. Innovation is more than the technical output (irrespective if that output is product or service orientated) and interventions at policy and enabling levels need to adapt and/or continue to prioritise infrastructural, ecosystem, and 'soft' people related initiatives and actions to ensure a balanced innovation support offering.

For IPACSO Innovation Framework - the respective outputs of the survey and interview data will directly input into shaping the core and supporting innovation modules The actual components and content of the IPACSO framework will, in turn be developed into decision support modules and associated toolkits which will be equally iteratively developed, trialed and validated with target stakeholder engagement, primarily through validation training Bootcamps and wider dissemination and outreach channels.

Furthermore, the research insights, and the IPACSO project overall, will have relevance to the European trust and security Framework research programme portfolio which are increasingly charged with focusing on potential innovation arising from their activities, in terms of increasing project outputs for economic and societal benefit.

References

1. EC, Cyber Security Strategy of the European union: An Open Safe and Secure Cyberspace (2013)
2. Maughan, D., Baleson, D., Lindqvist, U., Tudor, Z.: Crossing the "valley of death": transitioning cybersecurity research into practice. J. IEES Secur. Priv. **11**(2), 14–23 (2013)
3. Tidd, J.: A Review of Innovation Models Discussion Paper 1, Science and Technology Policy Research Unit, Tanaka Business School, University of Sussex (2006)
4. Dooly, Z., Galvin, S., Power, J., Renard, B., Seldeslachts, U.: IPACSO: towards developing an innovation framework for ICT innovators in the privacy and cybersecurity markets. In: Cleary, F., Felici, M. (eds.) Cyber Security and Privacy. LNCS, vol. 470, pp. 148–158. Springer, Heidelberg (2014)
5. Garud, R., Kumaraswamy, A., Sambamurthy, V.: Emergent by design: performance and transformation at infosys technologies. Organ. Sci. **1**(277), 277–286 (2006)
6. OSMOSIS, D2.1 Report on the Identified Security's Market Potential/ D2.2 Report on Taxonomy Definition (2010). http://www.osmosisecurity.eu/system/files/OSMOSIS_D2.1%20and%20D2.2_integrated.pdf
7. Rothwell, R.: Towards the fifth-generation innovation process. Int. Mark. Rev. **11**(1), 7–31 (1994)
8. Cormican, K., O'Sullivan, D.: Auditing Best Practice For Effective Product Innovation. Technovation **24**(10), 819–829 (2004)
9. Jacobs, D., Snijders, H.: Innovation Routine: How Managers can Support Repeated Innovation. Stitching Management Studies, Van Gorcum, Assen (2008)
10. Tidd, J.: A review of innovation models discussion paper 1. Science and Technology Policy Research Unit, Tanaka Business School, University of Sussex (2006)
11. Eleveens, C.: Innovation Management: A Literature Review of Innovation Process Models and their Implications. Nijmegen, NL (2010)
12. Rothwell, R.: Towards the fifth-generation innovation process. Int. Mark. Rev. **11**(1), 7–31 (1994)
13. Van de Ven, A., Angle, H., Poole, M.: Research on the Management of Innovation: The Minnesota studies. Harper & Row, New York (1989)
14. Cormican, K., O'Sullivan, D.: Auditing best practice for effective product innovation management. Technovation **24**, 819–829 (2004)
15. Tidd, J., Bessant, J., Pavitt, K.: Managing Innovation – Integrating Technological, Market and Organizational Change. Wiley, New York (2005)
16. World Economic Forum (WEF), Enhancing Europes Competitiveness- Fostering Innovation Driven Entrepreneurship in Europe (2014). http://www3.weforum.org/docs/WEF_Europe Competitiveness_InnovationDrivenEntrepreneurship_Report_2014.pdf

Author Index

Printed in the United States
By Bookmasters